Julian M. Watson was raised in a Cambridgeshire village and moved to Hampshire at 11 years of age. After leaving school he worked various jobs, computing, engineering at sea and on land, generally earning good money and having fun until his father decided that he should get a "steady" job. So he took on the job as rookie undertaker earning less than a quarter of his previous pay.

For Dan, the only person mad enough to see the seriously ridiculously strange things that go through my mind, thanks, and to dear Jenny who had the immense patience to put up with an ageing nit picking Virgo in restoring it to a digital form, thanks dear Jen.

Julian M. Watson

SO FAR SO WHAT!

Tales From Beside The Grave

AUSTIN MACAULEY PUBLISHERS™

LONDON * CAMBRIDGE * NEW YORK * SHARJAH

Copyright © Julian M. Watson 2024

The right of Julian M. Watson to be identified as author of this work has been asserted by the author in accordance with sections 77 and 78 of the Copyright, Designs and Patents Act 1988.

All rights reserved. No part of this publication may be reproduced, stored in a retrieval system, or transmitted in any form or by any means, electronic, mechanical, photocopying, recording, or otherwise, without the prior permission of the publishers.

Any person who commits any unauthorised act in relation to this publication may be liable to criminal prosecution and civil claims for damages.

All of the events in this memoir are true to the best of author's memory. The views expressed in this memoir are solely those of the author.

A CIP catalogue record for this title is available from the British Library.

ISBN 9781035855087 (Paperback)
ISBN 9781035855094 (ePub e-book)

www.austinmacauley.com

First Published 2024
Austin Macauley Publishers Ltd®
1 Canada Square
Canary Wharf
London
E14 5AA

Table of Contents

Preface	9
Chapter One: And in the Beginning	10
Chapter Two: The Knowledge	18
Chapter Three: More Learning	24
Chapter Four: Funerals of Different Religions	34
Chapter Five: Breakdowns	48
Chapter Six: The Public Mortuary	55
Chapter Seven: Nuts	66
Chapter Eight: The Delaney Mob	83
Chapter Nine: A Funny Thing That Happened to Me on the Way to the Crematorium	108
Chapter Ten: People, Places and Buildings	124
Chapter Eleven: Another Fine Mess!	136
Chapter Twelve: Don't Call the Pickfords!	146
Chapter Thirteen: D.I.Y. in Death?	173
The Po'face (or Postface)	178

Preface

This book is an account of my own experiences as a funeral director between 1976 and 1988. The persons mentioned are all real they are people that I have both laughed and cried with and as such are an unforgettable part of my life. Some of the people's names have been changed or omitted for reasons I think are better left unsaid.

Therefore, if I have used your name, be thankful. If not—be quiet!

Chapter One
And in the Beginning

And it came to pass in the year of our Lord, one thousand nine hundred and seventy-six, that a great pestilence was sent upon the land in the form of sun and warmth hitherto unheard of in the land.

And the father said unto the son, "Go forth and see to the shop and use your time to the good, drag up the business from the depths and make something of your life!"

I should explain that I was 26 years old and had spent the last eight years in various jobs from computing to engineering and had a rather idyllic life whereupon I would work on a contract somewhere and when it ended, have a few months off and some fun. This time, the few months had stretched out a little and I had spent some time with the old mum and dad, helping with boats for one and gardens for the other and having a great time with them both.

Well, that's enough of the prehistoric days' except to mention that the shop was an undertaker in 'Ackney' and I had been brought up in the stockbroker belt and me mum, w'o was brought up in 'Ackney', 'ad been an English Teacher and taught in Watford, they wouldn't let her teach in Harrow, in case she spelt it with an apostrophe.

The story so far:

Period A: Birth, an uncertain period of life which doctors agree with, is one of the most critical times.

Period B: The Begetting, this should be fun, if not, you've got something very wrong.

Period C: Death, an uncertain period of life which doctors agree is one of the most critical times after which all undertakers have a vested interest.

This, of course, is where we come in and provide a very useful service. In the year 1840, my great-great-grandfather, George Robert Moss, moved from the shires and took up residence in a smart and growing suburb of the north-east of London slap bang next to a public house, where he built up a respected and successful business that was eventually passed on to his son, George Robert, his son, Arthur Sidney, his nephew, George Robert and then to his brother-in-law, Bob. The last two being managers on behalf of my grandmother and mother.

Dear old uncle Bob, what a character, a diminutive little fellah with a heart of gold and as honest as the day is long, smoked like Kuwait, had very few teeth and even less hair. He and his wife had been managing the business since 1963 and most people in the area thought he was my dad, but he wasn't, he also wasn't my uncle but simply my mother's father's brother's son's wife's sister's husband. Got that? Questions will be asked.

Monday, 14 September 1976.

Suited, booted, washed, shaved and apprehensive, I presented myself for duty. Being the great-great-grandson of the founder, I was naturally expected to be able to drive a Rolls Royce and carry a coffin on my shoulder with no training whatsoever. I remembered that last funeral I had attended (and the first), it had been that of my grandmother, the wife of Arthur Sidney, who had been very close to our family as children and for whom I had a great affection.

Driving lesson—turn that, press that to start the engine, that's the gears, right pedal is 'go', left 'stop'. DO NOT drive into the hearse, let anything get between you and the hearse, get lost, damage anything, upset anyone or do anything generally wrong!

We wash and clean cars, load the coffin into the hearse and off to the house, 77 Evering Road, Stoke Newington—slap bang on a traffic light junction at the end of a very narrow one-way street—stopping outside the house we effectively block the street.

Dear old Bob, completely unperturbed as I point out the increasing tailback of traffic but the florist is late so they will have to wait! At this time a logical question came into my head, I told myself to keep quiet. Little did I know that some years later, I would be standing just around the corner conducting my first funeral when one of my own recruits would notice similar logic and fail to shut up!

Sometime later, the florist, apparently realising that sitting in a traffic jam was not getting his job done and that he was becoming increasingly late decided to seek a detour unto the residence being the object of his quest in delivery of floral tributes only to discover the reason for delay in vehicular progression. A short while later, the traffic, not unsurprisingly, began to flow normally once more.

Right pedal, go, left pedal stop, so far so good, all new roads to me, don't lose the hearse, don't hit the hearse and eventually and to my great relief, we arrive at the cemetery where I am directed with concise hand movements and the first part is over.

"Now," said Bob, "You'll be alright if you keep your shoulder under the box, it won't fall off!"

Who am I to argue with that, it seemed perfectly logical to me, what was worrying me, however, was firstly how was it going to get onto my shoulder, secondly, were my puny legs going to collapse under the strain and thirdly, when we had arrived at the place where one and two had been achieved, what then!

Well, here goes, up on the shoulder, so far so good, keep in step, so far so good and after a little weaving and staggering we arrive at the catafalque and bending slightly forward and the coffin slides from my shoulder and onto the rollers, hereby completing much calamitous things were to befall me.

One down—NEXT!

And so to Stevens Avenue with the late Audrey May Wicks.

This may be a good time to point out that a Rolls Royce limousine is not a small car and that some of the streets of Hackney were built for the 'Orse 'n' Cart and not very large ones at that, furthermore, the streets were also devoid of parked cars!

Now here I am, twenty-six years old, Jack the Lad, driving a Rolls Royce, been driving for nine years and had my share of newish and fast cars, driven some miles and to my mind, encountered every conceivable road hazard and gap there is and handled the lot whilst changing gear, rolling a cigarette and tuning the radio all at sixty miles per hour.

And now, this diminutive dwarf wants me to reverse this 40 acre limousine through the eye of a needle. "Give over!" but all he keeps saying is "Come on back, you're alright, on yer left, come on, keep 'er coming."

By doing as I was told and concentrating on what was happening on the driver's side by hanging my head out of the window and looking up and down, I developed Moss's theory of cars and gaps which came in very handy whilst attempting to train other drivers to perform similar feats in the years to come.

Moss's Theory of Gaps and Cars

If you leave the smallest safe gap on the side you can see by shoving your head out of the window and still hit the other side, there wasn't much chance of missing it in the first place. Using this theory only when the boss insists that the Bl**dy car will so parkinwell fit will always prove the boss at fault and cause the conversation to cease there and then!

Having performed said feat and extracted from the vehicle to see how close I was, only proved the boss to be well in the right and the car parked awkwardly towards the driver's side of the lane.

"Where to this time?" I ask his lordship.

"Same place!" said he.

Well, this should be easy, I think to myself, *Out of here, turn right, first left and first right, down past the playing fields, no problems*, nice and smoothly off we go and the hearse goes off in a completely different direction leaving me behind totally unprepared for a tight left-hand turn so that I had to reverse up to take another swing at it.

Slightly confused and following in and out of the back streets until we stop at this boarded-up corner shop whereupon, as I am about to switch off the engine, the hearse moves off again. More confused, I follow, whereupon the bearer, sitting next to me, calmly says that they probably used to own that shop. Thankfully, we now continue to the cemetery in a logical direction and, on arrival, I think to myself that I now know what to do when.

"Where's he going now?" I mutter.

"Other chapel, m' boy," said the bearer.

In we go and the only difference is that there are trestles instead of a catafalque, bow nicely and off to unload the flowers as before.

"Where are you goin', 'erbert?" said his lordship, whereupon I am informed that this is a burial. This morning was a cremation so we wait for the service to complete, coffin back in hearse and off to the graveside for another new experience, well, it's a nice day, hot, sunny, in fact, quite unlike England. Without incident, the coffin was loaded into the hearse, we proceeded to the graveside, lowered the coffin down into the grave, the flowers spread out for the mourners to see and all's well and off we go home again.

One down, I have now decided that since it was a cremation, the morning funeral was UP—Whatever next?

Back to the shop after dropping the mourners off, Stevens Avenue had miraculously become wider and both in and out were accomplished with minimal fuss.

"Park it up tight," he said. "We've got some running around to do, three removals!"

At this point, I realised that we had been taking highly polished and ornamented boxes of curious shape from a small room called a 'Chapel', sliding them into a Rolls Royce estate car, driving around the neighbourhood with some people who cried and doing the same trip in reverse but without the box! Thus, at some point, we were going to require more boxes or, more aptly, the inhabitants thereof.

Also, so far, I could see no reason for this to change, the hearse had always arrived back before the limousine, therefore parking at the back of the garage and closer to the chapel of rest and thus convenient for loading on the way out. Our garage was long and narrow and just less than nine feet wide with an uneven York flagstone floor and was the route of entry of our temporary residents via "closed vehicle and temporary coffin."

For the unenlightened, have you ever noticed those very clean and sometimes very old three-quarter-ton vans with suited individuals sitting in the front who are always laughing and joking…they are more than you think. The more modern idea is a plain white estate car with red crosses on the side, the rear windows painted white and the word 'AMBULANCE' adorning the sides and rear. I am uncertain whether this is meant to be more inconspicuous, however, the theory is that there is no Road Fund Licence required on an ambulance.

The 'Temporary Coffin' or shell, the theory is the same as that of the 'operation gown' in a hospital, one size and fits where it touches, manufactured in the shape of a coffin of strong glass fibre with strong handles at each end and lid held on by tough clips. They are either plain brown or grey to look unobtrusive, be functional, easy to clean, durable and light, which, as a general rule, they do.

But one thing that has always bothered me is why they are made in two different sizes. The large size is about 6'5" long and about 24" wide and there is usually one at about 5'10" for which the price is quoted and the large one is extra, of course, however, if one were to buy just one of each, one would thus be ensured of never having the right sized shell for the job at hand. Some years later,

I asked a salesman about this and was informed that they hardly ever sell the standard size.

The shell is moved about on a wheeled 'bier', a simple four wheeled device about the same height as the deck of the 'Closed Vehicle'. The wheels are trained at the same establishment as supermarket trolley wheels, therefore possessing the same magnetic attraction to vehicle bodywork. The frame of the bier is designed to fit snugly under the shell, which it does unless either the wheels are attracted to bodywork or relatives are watching when it will proceed to jostle the shell in any attempt to throw it to the ground. In this mode, it is in close liaison with the wheels.

This explained, it is a simple matter to imagine the problems that can arise with a six foot wide Rolls Royce, a two foot wide shell, an uneven floor and a garage of less than nine feet in width, especially if the car is badly parked or at least more than two inches from the wall. With the novice at the wheel again, it doesn't take much imagination.

"C'mon back, yer alright, on yer left, slower, right hand – STOP!!"

"Go forward on yer left, stop, now back on yer right."

And so on until, eventually they are satisfied, as I look at my handiwork and rate it a generous two out of ten compared with the old hand whose hearse is parked at a slight angle to avoid scuffing the tyres on the two-inch brick pier jutting out at the base of the wall in the dimly lit garage.

A quick and very welcome cup of tea provided by the manager's wife Winnie. "You've got a busy start on the job," she said and then we are off.

Three of us in the 'Closed Vehicle' with two shells in the back and I thought he said three removals. I counted mentally to myself, in this trade, you do not count on your fingers and certainly never lick them when reading your paper.

Our arrival at a four-storey estate in North Hackney we find distressed relatives waiting outside and we park the vehicle closest to the lift as Bob has a quick word with relatives and disappears upstairs. On his return, he looks at me with obvious concern. It is a very hot summer and the person awaiting our arrival has been dead for some several days on the top floor and the only thing that doesn't fit the norm is the fact that the lift is working.

"Have you got a strong stomach, boy?" he whispered to me.

Well, as I saw it, I would have to experience most things eventually and there is no time like the present so up we went with the shell in the lift.

Not a pretty sight and the odour, even less so. I do not know how much help I was but I think I did my bit in getting the old dear into the shell, but I do remember the perspiration running off me and the occasional scurry outside for a 'breath of fresh—'. On the way to the lift, we had to 'Strike' the shell, that is to say upend it to negotiate a bend in a corridor out through a doorway.

Houses are built to take all sorts of furniture pieces in its doorways but people only vertically.

The lift was added as an afterthought to this estate and was built for a maximum of four. Four who would have to be good friends with no leanings whatsoever to obesity or one removal shell and one other person.

As is normal with the carriage of the dead in most of the Christian world and protocol was always observed, the mode of travel is 'feet first', thus the person, who knew what to do and where we were going, not me, went first, taking the foot and arriving at the lift put his end down and with Bob helping me at my end we struck the shell again into the vertical position and began to reverse into the lift, the other two lifting the foot bit by bit whilst I provided vertical stability and what additional help I could whilst receiving minor contusions to the hands and fingers caught between shell and lift or wall and being occasionally assaulted by the lift door attempting to close.

At last mission accomplished, I'm in, the shell's in, at this moment, Bob's hand reaches round from the outside, presses the 'G' button and with a cheery "We'll see you at the bottom," the metal door grates slowly, slowly across the threshold to reach the far side with a metallic though not uneerie 'Clump'.

During the next two or three millennia, I leisurely scout my present universe, a three by three by seven foot stainless steel box containing me, a glass fibre box containing its unwitting occupant exuding unpleasant odours, a macabre spectre to my imagination. The other occupant chose this precise moment to move inside the shell. I spent the next eon telling myself not to scream, cry, panic, be sick or do anything else that might seem unprofessional and that somewhere in the other universe this had all happened before and that it was really quite normal. With a lurch, the lift then started its downward journey and the light went out.

It was, of course, a great relief when the lift came to a halt, but a little of a shock to three quarters of those involved when the door opened on the second floor and the couple waiting for the lift politely agreed to wait for the next car. Without further event, we continued our journey to the ground and with further minor contusions and portal assaults on me, our passenger was extracted from the lift and inserted into the vehicle.

Hyperventilation whilst attempting to hold one's breath, is an interesting state to attempt. "You alright, son?"

"Yes!" I stammered, lying.

And we were off to the next one, a dingy first floor room and a little old lady lying dead on the bed, nothing of her, poor old luv! We'll use the stretcher, they agree, the stretcher is a plasticised canvas affair with wooden slats to stiffen it, three handles on each side and three internal safety belts to stop the occupant from getting up. This is a very useful device for handling in confined spaces and especially down stairs, however, not the image on the street, so the stretcher goes inside the shell in the hallway.

Uneventfully, though not irreverently, our passenger was conveyed to the transport and then on to the public mortuary to drop our first passenger and being very glad to be rid of that one, even though temporarily. Suitably labelled and entered into the correct book and the pleasant smell of bleach to rinse out the shell before we are off to the Old Peoples home.

A cheerful matron meets us and thanks us for coming so promptly as she ushers us through the corridors, shows us the fire exit and, whilst unlocking an adjacent door, asks us if we could take him out through that way so that we wouldn't upset the others on their way to their dinner.

We enter a clean and tidy, fresh smelling room and there under a clean sheet on the bed, the slender frame of an elderly gent lying on a clean bed, eyes closed and with a small, rolled towel under his chin, holding his mouth shut. Calmly and quietly, we took the old gent back to our shop and unloaded our two passengers to our chapel and I realise how three into two does go as we had left one at the public mortuary.

After parking all the vehicles we begin our next tasks of cleaning and disinfecting where necessary, propping up heads and the like whereupon it was finishing time.

"You alright, boy?" said Bob.

"Yup," I lied.

"Don't be late in the morning. We've got an early Catholic, we're on the front at nine, Paddy's land at eleven, better be here by eight."

HERE ENDETH THE FIRST DAY!

Chapter Two
The Knowledge

During the remainder of that week, I learnt to fit and line coffins and yes, they do burn them, except, of course, on certain occasions when they bury them.

Most coffins today are made of chipboard, veneered to a very high quality with a hardwood such as oak, elm or mahogany and polished to a high gloss. Small funeral directors will normally buy a stock of readymade coffins from a large supplier and custom fit handles and linings to order, yes, they do burn them too, except, of course, on certain occasions, when they bury them, just as with the coffin.

Most coffin handles are made of plastic and plated with either nickel or brass to provide the shine. The coffin is lined with thin white plastic sheeting with the inside set with its frill and braids tacked in with a staple gun and finished with brass or chrome headed pins.

Before the invention of the staple gun and we must remember that there was life and death, before the advent of such marvels, 'gimp' pins were used, these little things were the cause of many a sore finger and certainly taught me how to use a tack hammer very, very accurately. The gimp pin was a small galvanised steel pin mass produced for the upholstery trade by a stamping process therefore, leaving lots of rough edges.

These little things were designed to cause maximum pain to one's pinkies on two counts, firstly, being less than half an inch long so as not to come through the coffin itself, they would disappear between thumb and index finger as the hammer approached.

The resultant pain caused by contact between hammer and digit being proportional to the inverse of the temperature of the workshop and secondly, if, by some miraculous chance, the hammer were to engage the head of the pin, one of the rough edges would tear painfully into flesh of thumb or forefinger allowing the red fluid to appear and stain the lining of the coffin in the most prominent place possible. This last escapade normally requiring replacement of the lining.

There are generally two kinds of linings for the average coffin, side sheets and gown, the latter with sleeves, gown and frill are fitted after the occupant, all items being separate, they are placed on the body and tucked inside each other to look right, this is possible only if the star of the show agrees not to move afterwards.

Murphy's Law of undertaking, of course, states that if anything can possibly go wrong, it will do so only at the most embarrassing moment. So using the maxim of "So far so good" is not recommended.

The clasping together of hands, no, not in prayer, in the coffin so that they stay together and look natural can be both time consuming and exasperating, shouting doesn't help and pleas of appeal to the other party can make one feel very silly when being observed by another member of staff. Various methods of securing have been tried including concealed string but none as successful as a cooperative corpse.

The side sheets are just about what they say, usually in satin and used to line the coffin when the body is being dressed in its own clothes and thereby hangs many an interesting tale.

Other things learnt over the first few days included the difference between coffin and casket. Apart from price, a coffin is a box designed for the conveyance of the deceased, naturally, but has shaped shoulders, the sort of thing popular in "Keep death off the roads" stickers and commercials. I have often wondered how those advertisers would view a working hearse from that context.

The curve at the shoulders is achieved by 'cuffing' whereby grooves are cut by a specially designed saw through about three quarters of the wood along about eighteen inches of the coffin side, allowing the smooth curve to be pulled in around the baseboard. The coffin having a flared foot. This is one of those strange things that we take for granted, at the foot of a coffin, the piece of wood across the end is angled out from the foot to the toe about twenty degrees, I have seen coffins made without this flare and they look very strange.

The casket, probably an American idea, in contrast, is a simple rectangular box, both coffin suppliers and funeral directors delight in charging extra money for. Cemeteries also justify making an extra charge for digging a rectangular hole for a casket as opposed to digging a rectangular hole for a coffin. Some years later, I asked Mr Willis why this was; he took me to one side and secretly admitted that they like the extra money.

I had learnt the difference between public and private graves, a private interment cost more and gave exclusive use of the plot to the purchaser for an infinite or specified time and allowed the purchaser to erect memorials of their choice according to certain rules and regulations until they changed the rules and regulations.

The public interment or unpurchased grave to distinguish it from a pauper's grave, is a large hole in the ground, where unrelated people are buried, in coffins and caskets and separated by a minimum depth of earth as distinct from the paupers grave which is a large hole in the ground, where unrelated people are buried, in coffins and caskets are separated by a minimum depth of earth. Since there are no longer any paupers in England, providing them a specific class of people with their own burial service has ceased.

I have now attended cremations and burials, both public and private interments but only one church service, Catholic.

Catholic services nearly always include a full mass said in church and although the Catholic funeral service is very short, the additional forty minute mass, coming and going in and out, to and from the church, makes the whole funeral a much lengthier affair. For the funeral director and his staff, the vital actions are essentially the same as for any other funeral except that the likelihood of getting wet, even on a sunny day, is increased.

I believe that somewhere along the development of the Catholic faith, there was a drought. The value of water therefore increased, the Church, being the church and above mortal pestilences and famines, must therefore have maintained the right to throw it about at their own free will, at dead bodies, coffins, coffin conveying carriages and in holes in the ground. Various methods of Aqua Deus dispersal have been devised over the ages and all of these seem to uphold my theory of drought since John the Baptist's approach has been long abandoned in favour of the token few drops.

The most ancient method in current use is the brush method, soft brush hairs about the same quantity as a household one inch paint brush are sealed in the end of a polished brass handle, this being dipped in a brass bowl full of water and the brush being ceremoniously flicked at the body/coffin/hearse/hole to bless and purify, however, unsuspecting bearers have been caught in the crossfire on many occasions.

I have up till now assumed that this was accidental but it may have been a futile attempt at purification since most of the bearers I have met would put fire and brimstone to shame. The resultant dowsing is not too bad on a hot sunny day, but on a frosty morning with the prospect of the next forty minutes standing outside, grumbles abound.

Novice priests are the worst offenders as they tend to be overzealous. Luckily, it is not usually long before some kind-hearted sixteen-stone bearer will come to the rescue with a friendly word:

"Listen son, we're all doin' our job 'ere. I know, but if any of that filthy water gets on my clean shirt today, you're gonna be sprinklin' water from an unusual orifice. Do we understand each other?" Such a helpful lot, we can all use a friendly piece of advice now and again.

Other methods of water disposal are a similar handle with a small, perforated sphere at the end filled with some sort of metal gauze. This again is dipped in the bowl and similarly flicked and holds the record for the most rusty marks on the shirt.

With the advent of the age of plastics, another sprinkler system has evolved, working on the same principal as the plastic lemon, shaped in the form of Their Lady but not yellow. I find it somewhat irreverent for Their Lady to be grasped firmly in the priest's hand and squeezed so that a jet of water, though holy, would dart from the top of her head. The jet, naturally, goes anywhere but the direction of aim and usually in the direction of the sixteen stone bearer, "Now Listen, son!"

Times for bearers to beware are, on being received into church, after the service when the coffin is replaced in the hearse, this one is great when you have just had a long heavy carry, slipped the box thankfully onto the rollers of the deck of the hearse and as you turn round to take a deep breath, splash, straight in the face, then as you go about your duties, the mourners wonder why you've been crying.

To add further confusion the last case can change without proper notice and this is where experience helps, on rainy days, it is good procedure for the experienced bearer to notice whether the priest has left his umbrella at the church door or is carrying it as the procession leaves from the nave, if not, caution is advised. On foresight, may suddenly decide to bless the coffin there and then and swing round, scattering holy water in all directions.

Finally, at the graveside, the priest might turn to the funeral director and ask whether the ground has been consecrated.

"Er—Yup!" being the usual response.

Further holy water is sprinkled in case the 'Yup' was negative and the committal proceeds with further sprinklings.

The sprinklers, brush or sphere type are then handed around the relatives to further sprinkle holy water in memory of their lost loved one. For some unknown reason, I have never seen a priest part with his precious plastic version for relatives to squeeze.

One day, however, we discovered a Catholic lemon squeezer under the seat in the hearse, full of the sacred water. This came in useful on many occasions when priests might turn up without. Amazing stuff that holy water, that bottle remained in the hearse for many years and to my knowledge, only came out at cemeteries to be passed round priests and relatives and then back into the glove compartment, but it never ran out!

Some priests choose to say a decad of the Rosary at the graveside, this would entail the chant from the priest, "Holy Mary, Mother of God, blessed art thou and blessed art the fruit of Thy womb, Jesus," followed by a similar chant from the gathered congregation, the priest would then repeat his chant a further nine times, thus making ten or decad.

It is easy to imagine how difficult it is to remember the number of times this has been said so that different priests have different methods of keeping a tally. Luckily, Christians are supplied from birth with half on each hand so that folding a finger over at the beginning of each chant and going though both hands will usually provide the required number.

Another method employed by one particular priest used five small pebbles. At the beginning of each chant, one stone was passed from one hand to the other and then back to the first hand, candidly behind his back, I was often standing next to or behind the priest at the time of the committal and would notice these happenings. After the decad was said, the pebbles would be quietly slipped into a convenient pocket to be ready for the next time. One day, when driving the first limousine back myself with the priest sat beside me, my sense of humour got the better of me.

"I see you've lost a stone, Father."

"Oh, very kind of you to notice, I'm trying to cut down on the fatty foods," said the priest.

"No, Father, not weight. You were two rounds short of your decad today. Have you lost a **pebble**, is what I meant."

He felt in his pocket and counted out the five stones.

"No, they are all there," he said, looking worried. "Did I only say eight?"

"Well, I wasn't consciously counting from the start, but I think I started from about number three and I only got to five when you finished. I also thought it was over rather quickly as well."

"Oh dear, I wonder whether anyone else noticed," questioned the priest rather agitatedly.

"Oh, dear!"

"Do you mean down here or up there?" I asked, nodding skywards and immediately regretted it as a frown appeared on his face.

"Do you always count them?" he replied to clear the air.

"Sometimes I've counted quite a few wrong ones," I offered. "But never an eight," I added, as an observation.

He was much more put out by the fact than I had imagined, but the worst of it was that although what I had said was perfectly correct, I was not absolutely certain that I had started counting at number three. During the following years, when we were together at funerals, he would always ask, "How was that?"

"Smack on, right on the nose," was the only reply I ever gave, whether I had been counting or not.

Chapter Three
More Learning

Two weeks before my return to the shop later the same year, I had the misfortune to be caught up in a fight in South West London and sustained not only facial injury but also damage to my right shoulder from being pushed through a plate glass window. This hurt, but also meant that for the foreseeable future, I would have to rely on my left arm and shoulder for lifting and carrying coffins.

In the undertaking world, this can be most annoying as a large number of the bearers tend to be older men, many of whom have similar troubles, therefore starting off with this handicap can cause problems when trying to match up bearers.

Coffins are generally carried with three bearers on the three-legged stool principal, thus maintaining even weight on all bearers at all times, over uneven ground and up and down stairs. The shortest bearer being at the front (foot), tallest at the back (head). If only two of your bearers can only carry on one shoulder, for instance, one left and one right and the other bearer is of a height in between the monoscapulatic bearers, there is a problem and vice versa.

This can result in a little huddle of bearers arriving at the cemetery, walking to the business end of the hearse and apparently entering into some sort of pantomime changing places and gesturing of hands whilst they decide who will carry and in what position until, at last, the coffin is borne aloft and on its way.

Ideally, one chooses one's staff to be perfectly matched in height and gait. The world not being perfect and bearer cloning not a current practice, we have to take what comes and other attributes take preference, like driving records and licences.

Shouldering a coffin is surprisingly easy, especially with three bearers and a new man can easily be 'carried' by two experienced men. The 'foot' man must be experienced and allow for taking corners either tight or wide according to direction of the turn, the other experienced man providing sideways force on the coffin to push the new man left and right leaving the new man to concentrate on, staying under the coffin, upright, where his foot is going next, what is going to happen when they get to their destination and panicking in any available spare moment.

Needless to mention, two experienced men can make the novice's job very easy and alternatively extremely difficult and uncomfortable, should the young lad become too large for his footwear. The over exuberant young lad who plays the odd trick on the old hands around the garage and workshops can find himself carrying a coffin at the cemetery being the only bearer to scrape his thighs and shins on ageing, gravestones and trudging through muddy puddles whilst his colleagues will make the course unscathed.

A favourite trick that is often played on the rookie, best in April because of the showers, the stronger the better because, not only does the game have more effect to the recipient and give most pleasure to the perpetrators but also most easy to arrange and carry out.

The requirements are church service, hearse, a deluge at the right time and a quantity of very bad and mischievous sense of humour from all the old hands.

The rear and loading doors of nearly all hearses open and swing upward, being coach built, the glass should fit well and be free of leaks.

With any luck, it will be raining as the cortege arrives and the prospective perpetrators will see the possibility of the dirty deed and leave the back door in the horizontal position. It is necessary to be helpful to the rookie and to make sure that he keeps dry during the duration of the service, as this makes future requests more logical. It may therefore mean that the old hands may have to suffer a small amount of discomfort.

All being well, the service will end, the sun will have come out and dried the roads and it will be generally April. The coffin, having been loaded into the hearse, will solicit an unusual request and statement from the 'farmer' of the game.

"Ere son, if I load your car, I can stand in this sun to dry my coat, it got wet in that deluge. Oh yes, you were alright standing well on the porch. Look, you're not even damp. You go into the church and get the trestles and put them in the hearse."

The lad, having been coerced and made to feel guilty letting his mates get wet whilst he stayed dry, politely squeezes past the mourners scoots up the altar rail, collects the trestles and then had to patiently follow the last of the mourners out of the church.

Now, we are waiting for him. Usually, a quick nod to put the trestles in the back of the hearse already open and waiting for him will relay the urgency required. At this time the lad should be the only person at the back of the hearse, standing in the warm sun, nice and dry.

Hopefully hurrying, he will pull down the back door of the hearse, which, brimming with its cargo of clear water that will continue its earthward journey whilst gaining momentum as the slope of the door is quickly increased. Sometimes, the 'farmer' and friends will glimpse the look of awful realisation on the poor lad's face as he remembers the rain, hears the initial slosh of water and looks up to receive the unavoidable reward of his colleagues light hearted fun.

Now comes the hard part. For the experienced bearer/perpetrator or 'farmer', keeping a straight face on the way to the cemetery can be very, very difficult. There was only one man I ever knew, Graham, who had sufficient control to then wipe down the benign creature with a miraculously available chamois leather whilst saying, "Now, look, you've got yourself all wet," just as a doting mother might do to a grubby son returning from a bicycle ride.

Well worthy of a mention at this point is the integrity of nearly all staff I met in my years as an undertaker. Whilst the lads would laugh and joke at the most ghastly and bizarre occurrences and tasks required of them, there was a good feeling of care and respect for the dead at all times. The seemingly hard and heartless things are said in jest as an ego boost to overcome a difficult situation, either for themselves or for one of their colleagues. Not having been to war, thankfully, I can imagine that similar gruesome humour arising to cope with the awful scenes in the trenches of the recent wars.

With the approach of Christmas and winter, a good healthy cremation was far preferable to a cold muddy graveside. Even with cremation, handling those wet floral wreaths on a frosty morning was enough to give anyone the agonies of frostbite and let us not forget the many times we have caught our fingers in the wires whilst tying those wreaths down on top of the hearse with a howling gale blowing sleet in one ear, the resultant melted water trickling down one's neck.

Florists are a wonderful bunch of tradesmen and probably as equally helpful or not so as any other group of professionals. Traditionally the base of a wreath is a wire frame onto which is strapped the discarded leaves, stalks and foliage from floral displays, this done with florist's wire. The chosen blooms then have their stalks cut short and wired onto the base. The result was a solid object which would hold enough water to keep the flowers fresh for a reasonable length of time and be sturdy enough to take a reasonable amount of handling and strapping down on the roof of the hearse.

As with everything that works well and uses all the raw material, it is obviously doomed and floristry is no exception to the rule. With the invention of the 'oasis' water retaining foam, it was possible to order large expanses of the material, cut it to shape, cover it with wrapping paper and stick flowers into it anywhere and they stay after a fashion. The result is a light, fragile item that falls apart at the first opportunity, fails to hold blooms in place and is extremely prone to being blown about by virtue of its very light weight. Furthermore, the florist is left with any amount of waste stalks and foliage to dispose of.

When mourners purchase their floral tributes, they are generally in some state of shock and tend to go "over the top" with the size of the tributes and, if not warned by the helpful florist, will cause the funeral director some headaches on the day of the funeral. The words 'MUM' and 'DAD' are fine but 'GRANDAD' is seven letters and being about twelve inches high will make the whole tribute about seven feet long. We very often learn that grandad and grandchild had a very close relationship and would seem rather fitting to have the child's wreath, only placed on the coffin, thus saving arguments between bickering sons and daughters.

Grandad being five foot nothing in his stocking feet, parked his hobnails many years before and having had a snug fitting coffin fitted for the great day, tact comes into play when the thankless funeral director has to point out that the coffin is only five feet eight long and the grave will therefore only be six feet and that their beautiful floral tribute would not only overhang the coffin but was already and would continue to be a downright bloody nuisance since the deck of the hearse was only six feet nine, anyway!

Calmly suggesting that the tasteful three foot cross and the lovely pillow would look just right on the coffin, we discover from the dagger glares that these sensible items are from Donald and Edna and they haven't spoken to the family since that unmentionable day in nineteen-forty-eight and nobody can quite understand why they bothered to show up unless it was just to gloat!

The style of floral tributes are many and varied and provided that relatives and the florist liaise with the funeral director on the unusual pieces everything goes fine and I have handled some wonderful works of art such as football pitches complete with goalposts, players in the correct strip and even the grandstands, a motorcycle that measured three feet long, grand pianos and an assortment of other musical instruments, dogs, cats, foaming pint pots as well as the normal hearts, pillows, gates of heaven, names and the ridiculous chair.

The chair as a floral tribute is the worst to handle of the normal pieces, usually bought by a close relative and required to take its correct place in the hierarchy of proximity to the coffin, it is too tall to stand up in the hearse window, too deep to stand at the head of the coffin on the deck and too flimsy to be strapped down on the top of the hearse and survive the journey to the cemetery in view of the imminent raging storm. The normal way around this is to hope that there is another chair or gate of heaven that can be strapped to the back.

On some occasions, especially when the funeral is to start early and the florist has a large order to fill, he may ask whether the flowers can be delivered to the funeral directors premises on the day before the funeral, this can be very useful as the display on the hearse can be arranged and secured prior to leaving the shop.

I remember one such occasion when we were very glad to be able to dress the hearse in the shelter of the garage in view of the driving sleet of that morning and after congratulating ourselves on the work of art, including the firm securing of a large floral canine in prominent position in the front row on top of the hearse, proceeded to drive out of the garage only to hear a dull thud as the lintel of the garage door gave the canine masterpiece a very unhealthy blow to the head. Whilst being very well made, it had not been designed to take such treatment. It was slaughtered!

Being due to collect the mourners within the next thirty minutes, we had a major rebuild job on our hands, apprentice floristry in ten minutes was the order of the day. Bending the little fella's frame straight was achieved to a degree and then proceeding to steal undamaged blooms from concealed places on his torso to replace the petal free counterparts on the mangled mutt's head. We were unable to select blooms from other pieces as the whole thing had been sprayed to colour.

We had done our best and off we went, praying that the sleet would continue in its ferocity to keep prying eyes from the unintended 'masterpiece' and send them back to the cars immediately after the service. Arriving at the cemetery, flowers out on a grassy bank where the cars would pass by on leaving the grave or on the far side of a muddy, puddled path. The flora was admired from afar!

A story from another funeral director of floral disaster, which was luckily understood by the mourners, was with hearse bedecked with flowers travelling along a dual carriageway in the north of London on a particularly windy day when a freak gust caught hold of all the sheaves and wreaths and deposited them unceremoniously across both adjacent lane and carriageway in the paths of passing traffic. When the traffic was eventually stopped, it was only possible to retrieve some of the sodden message cards, the remainder of the many pounds worth of tributes having been trampled under a juggernaut.

Mondays were always the worst for flowers as there is no fresh flower market on Sunday nights so the blooms are weekend leftovers, windy Mondays especially, when if not careful, the cortege could arrive at the cemetery with the odd few stalks where the chrysanthemums had been. Amusing for some, I must admit.

Fitting a large number of floral tributes into a limited space is an art in itself and therefore learning to dress a hearse comes with watching and practice. One learns that a small spray can be neatly dropped inside a round wreath, either on top or inside the hearse, making the resultant duo look the same as a much more grand wreath. Then at the cemetery, one learns that picking up the round wreath first pulls all the blooms out of the small spray, followed by a lesson in floristry.

Working as a team when loading the hearse is important with the funeral director at one end of the chain handing wreaths to the bearers with instructions for their placement whilst at the other end of the chain is the hearse driver trying to decipher the Chinese whispers with varied results.

During my time, the best team I had was Frank as hearse driver and Eddie in the limousine. Frank would try to create a symmetrical look from all directions, even from the top, for the benefit of those watching from upstairs windows whilst Eddie could load a whole lift full of flowers and remember whose piece went where. Various disagreements would arise at the ground floor but it usually looked good.

Driving around in large black shiny vehicles in a nice suit and clean white shirt is the side of the job most apparent to the public. This seems to be not too bad an occupation, but as with any trade, doing a job well makes it look easy and I can assure you that driving a hearse or limousine well takes a great deal of practice and concentration. Knowledge of the route, traffic light sequences, bus routes is a great help and for the hearse driver to keep the cortege moving steadily through the maze and keeping count of the cars behind, whilst the limousine drivers jobs is very similar but keeping up about six to ten feet behind the hearse so as not to let other cars push in which they will try to do with amazing regularity.

Good drivers pride themselves on their smoothness of driving coupled with their past record of not having let other cars break up the procession although I have seen a procession making its way with the hearse followed by the first two limousines, then a milk float and the other two limousines trying desperately to pass whilst keeping any number of private cars following, together.

At this point, if the hearse driver has not noticed the rogue vehicle in the midst, the situation is in danger of getting worse (and/or funnier). The 'lost' limousine drivers will probably be a hired driver and may not know where the church is and may have to ask the mourners causing upset and anguish or he will know where the cemetery is and if not able to find the cortege within a few moments of getting past the obstacle may decide to make his own way to the cemetery. This has occurred with the 'lost' limousine arriving both at wrong cemeteries when a sharp dash across town is required and also arriving at the right cemetery before the hearse.

Another scenario which has occurred many times is that the private cars, having become separated from the main cortege, will then follow any available passing funeral. In an area such as East London where there are as many as six cemeteries within a very small area, it is not unheard of to lose mourners altogether and similarly end up with complete strangers following you through the cemetery gates. At the chapel, people peer curiously at each other until one of the strangers will approach and ask, "Is this the funeral for James Smith?"

It is not usually very difficult to put them on the right track albeit late. On one occasion, I was asked a similar question after a full church service, only to be told, "We thought it was wrong as old Tom was an atheist, but we didn't like to walk out once the service had begun!"

It is easy to make mistakes in East London as three of the larger cemeteries are: The City of London Cemetery in Manor Park, The Manor Park Cemetery in Forest Gate and The East London Cemetery, also in Forest Gate. Dealing with people who have, luckily, only ever been to one funeral in their lives with the cemetery in East London can therefore lead to some confusion.

Cyclists can cause just as much annoyance in traffic as with any person driving. Whilst the cyclist is avoiding potholes weaving to and from the kerbside and there is oncoming traffic, the driver is loath to pass in case of accident. This is another way that a funeral cortege can be split up and again as with driving any vehicle, it can often happen that the cyclist will pass by on the left side when vehicle is stopped in traffic and as the traffic moves off the car will be delayed until he can eventually pass the cyclist only to be stopped in traffic again allowing the cyclist to pass by again.

One such incident, I remember, this had been happening with the cyclist pushing his way in between hearse and limousine, although the records do not show how many times. The driver of the limousine, a large sixteen-stone kind-hearted sort of fellow affectionately known as 'mad dog' was reported to have climbed down from his vehicle, knocked the cyclist out with a single blow, climbed back in the limousine and driven on without a word. Whilst this story has not been verified, one can only wonder exactly what the mourners would have thought but also be assured that they would be on their very best behaviour for the rest of their journey!

Most small funeral directors will have their own hearse and one or maybe two limousines, any additional requirements will have to be hired from outside. Hire cars and drivers can be obtained in a number of ways and from far and wide in an emergency.

Normally with the first call to your local limousine service, who will do his best to find a car for you from other local funeral directors if not available from his own fleet. This results in a friendly camaraderie amongst most of the staff in an area and a useful insight into other people's methods. Most funeral will need one or two limousines, although, very rarely, any number can be ordered and the largest I have ever been on is two hearses (one floral) and twelve limousines.

In that case, the cars arrived at the funeral directors premises stretching to the end of the block and around the corner. As with every trade, there is a hierarchy and the lowly little inexperienced me was always pushed to the back, probably so that if I did anything wrong, it wouldn't be to an important mourner. We arrived at the house where were assembled a herd of mourners and a sea of flowers. This, I realised, was going to be quite an experience.

The flowers were loaded onto two hearses and the roofs and luggage racks of some of the limousines and mourners were sat in place after much swapping. "No, uncle George should be in the next car back and little Timmy should be in this car, aunty Fred was going to drive himself and pick up cousin Chris from the station on the way; Oh hello Chris, well you will have to sit with Charmaine in car seven or are you still not on speaking terms, Oh good, well I suppose the next time we meet will be the wedding, congratulations. Now I must find aunt Cecelia!"

All seated and off we go, well off goes the hearse, some considerable time later, the car in front of me zooms off at a great rate of knots. This is where limousine driving becomes a very exacting and precise art. First some mathematics, two hearses and twelve limousines at about twenty feet long each will take some two hundred and eighty feet of parking space. If we allow one second between each vehicle beginning to move, the last vehicle will only be able to start moving fourteen seconds after the first. In the first quarter minute, the first vehicle will probably have accelerated to fifteen miles per hour and travelled over a hundred yards.

At this time the driver of the last limousine has to do some catching up, as do all the other drivers, to a lesser degree. As with all other funeral processions, the object is to stay together and at the back of the cortege, one will probably exceed forty miles per hour on many occasions, be driving with right foot firmly planted on the go pedal and never ever see a green traffic light, whilst the hearse travels along at a stately fifteen miles per hour.

School crossing ladies are a positive liability as they will tend to march out into the road with their magic wand as soon as they have assembled the required number of brats, regardless of the type of traffic passing. I must exclude one lollipop lady in particular, as we had buried her husband, who would always give us a cheery smile as we passed.

Arriving at the church and being pleased with myself, I unloaded my passengers taking a careful note of them to be able to recognise them later, as with foreigners and ducks, I like ducks, all limousines and drivers will look the same to the mourners. At the end of the service, it is the driver's job to round up his flock and insert them into his car, kiddy locks are a boon here, because once in, they cannot decide to play swapping again. And off to the cemetery at the same speeds and any colour but green lights. After the committal, things usually become more relaxed and the journey home is not so fraught and stopping at red traffic lights is not so frowned upon by the funeral director.

Being at the head of a large cortege has its headaches and humour as the traffic lights change from green and noticing the tail end Charlie careering along with eyes darting everywhere and trying not to shake his load about.

One day, it was tail end Billy whilst making our way westwards along the City Road to Great Portland Street after a funeral in one of the East End cemeteries. City Road is two lanes in each direction with traffic islands at various intervals, it was a very hot, sticky day so all the windows were open. In the left lane was a juggernaut grumbling its way along, belching forth foul fumes.

As first car, I decided there was enough time for all three limousines to pass the beast before the next turn so I began to pass. All went well until the truck approached a cyclist hitherto hidden from my sight. I was also fast approaching a traffic island on my right. With plenty of power in reserve, I accelerated past and so did the car behind as the truck began to slowly but surely pull out to pass the cyclist.

I watched in my mirror to see Billy's car suddenly swerve around the right-hand side of the traffic island and, in an instant, back into line with the other two cars. On our arrival at our destination, Billy was quite calm. However, his passengers were still a little more than agitated. They still vividly remembered the incident of the maniac white haired driver some ten years later.

———————————————————

Chapter Four
Funerals of Different Religions

It is necessary for the funeral director to know the rites of many different religions, races and creeds so that on initial contact, enough time is allotted for the service, funeral and preparations.

At our shop, the most common funeral we were called upon to arrange was for the West Indian community, be it Anglican, Catholic, Methodist or whatever.

The West Indian attitude to death is most refreshingly unselfish. Friends and relatives support the immediate family to a high degree, help them to let their grief out and give more vocal support to the belief that the deceased has gone to a better place. At the funeral, there is always a great deal more rousing hymn singing, emotion and physical embracing than at any of their stiff upper lipped white English counterparts. From a practical point of view, this does seem to be necessary, as from my observations, West Indian residents of our area would seem to die at a comparatively early age, leaving much younger families.

Whilst the funeral itself will take the same form as any other, there are some additional features involved, the first of which is that the family, friends and neighbours will always want to view the deceased to pay their last respects. It will be necessary to dress the body, not just favourite shirt, slacks and slippers but complete walking out Sunday best.

We now come to our first problem. When people die, they have usually been ill for some period of time. This often involves a lengthy stay in hospital, hospice or similar situation with usually a not inconsiderable loss of weight. The undertaker will often collect the body and make his preparations, including coffin and preservative treatments, allowing a little extra space in the coffin or casket for additional clothing when the Sunday suit will turn up large enough for two of the old boy.

Whilst this is better than the other way about, it still takes some artistic licence to hide the excess folds of clothing so that the result does not look as if it has just escaped from Oxfam.

I shudder to think what some of the relatives would have thought had they seen us making some of the alterations we did to the clothing that had been so lovingly prepared just to make them fit!

On the other side of the coin, there are those whose life just comes to an end quite suddenly often giving the undertakers a different problem. It is quite normal for some people not to have worn a suit for some length of time, many years maybe and to have put on some considerable amount of weight. The undertaker will make his preparations as normal to be presented with clothing that will go nowhere near doing its duty. This presents much more of a problem than the opposite and a degree in tailoring would be useful. Threads and strings underneath the body are used to hold clothing together that have been cut at the back in order to look right at the front.

In church, we would always hope that nothing would show or break revealing trade secrets.

With any luck and in a good number of cases, the clothes would fit reasonably well but here we come to the problem of the arms. Lie flat on your back and ask somebody else to put your shirt on for you. One arm is easy. Similar entertainment can be had with the jacket. Finally, we come to the gloves, white, always. Ask a friend to hold their hand completely limp and then put a glove on it. If that is too easy, dampen the hand and you will get some idea of the problems involved.

Women, on the other hand, are often much easier as they wear fewer articles of clothing. Sometimes we were presented with the most beautifully made funeral gowns, which simply laced up at the back for ease of fitment. There was someone locally who made funeral gowns to order complete with bonnet and gloves and they were the easiest things to fit and always looked the best. Women, however, who were dressed in their own clothing suffered the same problems as the men.

On one occasion and it is always with the wind lashing the rain against the windows on a cold dark night, late and with large things preparing to 'BUMP'. I was inside our workshop, alone, dressing a large gent of very firm build who just about fitted his clothing. Having taken some considerable time and effort in to get to the underwear and shirt stage, the gent's huge hands kept getting in the way as I was trying to put on his trousers. This is achieved quite simply up to the knees but then the fun starts.

Reaching over the body and rolling the hips toward you with one hand whilst pulling trousers up with the other hand, then walking round the other side of the body and repeating the process until the waistband is up to the waist. During this operation, I had placed both arms upwards out of the way with upper arms straight out from the torso with lower arms and hands at right angles so that the hands were above the head. Since the gent was solid and muscular, the hands were hanging in mid-air whilst I was heaving him about elsewhere.

I was finally tucking the shirt into the trouser as the arm on the side that I was working must have been disturbed by my pulling and pushing and overbalanced from its hanging position. Unbeknown to me, it is towards its normal "at rest" position by his side. Coming to an abrupt halt in the region of my posterior caused a little more than surprise, since I know that I was the only living person in the room.

Even though this was the sort of trick one of the lads might pull, I knew that all the doors were locked from the inside. I turned around to look over my shoulder with a little more than just a casual glance, missing more than one heartbeat. Breathing a sigh of relief, I continued my task.

Presentation completed, we could then expect a constant stream of friends and relatives coming to pay their last respects in our chapel of rest right through to the time of the funeral.

On the day of the funeral arriving in the street of the West Indian home, it was always a very easy matter to pick the right house since people had usually been arriving for some time, bringing flowers and congregating in the street. Sometimes getting through this melee of people to greet the family and find the immediate family flowers and where they should be placed was a matter of squeezing past many standing in the hallways.

Arriving in the parlour to find a sea of people picking their way amongst an ocean of flowers would present other problems. All these flowers then had to be transported to their correct places on hearse and cars until eventually, with all loaded, the next task would be getting the right people in the right cars. It was quite normal on such days with some of the narrow streets we worked to block the road completely.

When the time came to move, it would be quite common for a good number of the private cars to be facing the wrong way. By virtue of the great number of cars involved, a seemingly endless amount of reversing and turning would be necessary before the procession would be smoothly on its way.

An unforgettable day in Clapton Park was when two large funerals were begun in the same street at about the same time by two different funeral directors. A quick word with the other conductor and jockeying of funeral cars ensured that we would leave in different directions but I am still not sure how many mourners in their own cars followed the wrong procession.

At the church, the service could be anything between forty-five minutes and three hours, during which time the coffin was normally opened. The congregation, at the end of the service, would file past and pay their last respects.

At the cemetery, the committal would be accompanied by more hymns and the grave would be filled, mounded up and the flowers places on the grave before leaving. The filling of the grave is traditionally done by hand with all the attending men taking turns until the task was completed; the women would attend to the flowers. This custom continues and the funeral director therefore has to allow time for this to be done. However, in England's green and pleasant, rain may often bring on the seconds, there being mechanical diggers and the cemetery staff to cope with often very muddy ground.

As a result, dealing with a funeral of this type can take several hours more than a simple cremation but seems a better end to a life than just the handful that attend so many funerals.

With all the different sects of various religions, there are churches in many varying different types of buildings. One hall in Stoke Newington has a low ceiling with an even lower beam across the hall supporting the roof. Carrying a tail sided casket into this church took extra care, when normally, the bearers would carry with eyes cast respectfully down, one day the casket came to a sudden halt with a loud thud, the minister and organist halted in mid-flow and the stunned silence, broken by the funeral director's calm, "A little lower please gentlemen!"

Disaster can occur to flowers on coffins if great care and lookout is not maintained.

Another church hall in Hoxton is on the top floor of an old factory building with an impossibly narrow staircase for carrying any coffin with dignity. Luckily, there is a wide fire escape at the back of the building, so whilst the pastor and mourners file up the main staircase, the hearse drives to the rear of the building and the coffin is manhandled up the very steep noisy metal steps with the usual moaning and groaning from the staff.

"Up there? You must be joking."

"Do you know how heavy this thing is?"

"What if we drop it?" and other daft questions.

The answers naturally being, "Yes, I am not, yes and don't!"

The other different style of funeral we became most used to was from the Indian continent being the Hindu and Sikh religions. From our point of view, the difference in ceremony here was that the Sikh funeral always went via temple. Otherwise, the service we provided was the same. Method of disposal was always by cremation and usually as quickly as possible after death.

Most religious trends and traditions stem from some historic necessity and it would seem logical that in the Indian sub-continent, being hot, prompt disposal of the remains would save any likelihood of spreading disease from the dead to the living.

It is for similar reasons, some religions have strict dietary rules and steer clear of eating some sorts of meats, Similarly, in England, the tradition of eating oysters only when there is an "R" in the month, I will not eat an oyster if there is an "A" in the day.

The Indian religions caused me the greatest number of "near misses" in my entire career. Whilst trying to help out as much as possible by being as flexible as I could by pulling the few strings I had as much as I dared, I found myself walking a tightrope between time and the law on more than a few occasions.

Firstly, with cremation, doctors' papers are required. These forms are in essence quite simple, although certain legal formalities have to be observed. The reason for their existence is to be doubly sure that cause of death is agreed upon by two independent doctors as future investigations cannot be performed on cremated remains. If these forms cannot for any number of reasons be completed by the first doctor, the coroner's office will have to be informed and a 'postmortem' examination will have to be performed whereupon, the coroner will issue the form for cremation, all very simple.

The first doctor should be the doctor who has attended the deceased during their last illness, this being the same person who signed the certificate that the relatives will take to the Registrar of Births, Marriages and Deaths to register the death. The second doctor simply has to agree with the first and fill in a form to state such, for simplicity's sake. Both doctors have to see the body after death, this is the law. In hospital, this might seem straightforward; however, there are a number of ways in which a simple situation can become very out of hand.

If a death occurs during the night, the patient's hospital doctor may be off duty but be able to sign the registrar's form on the reports of nursing staff attending the death. Therefore, the doctor has not seen the deceased after death, although the death was not unexpected.

It is now possible for that doctor to be having some time off, going on holiday or generally being unavailable for the next few days. By the time the relatives have been summoned to the hospital, sent to the town hall and sat in queues for most of the day and lastly arrived at the undertakers to make arrangements, the first doctor could easily be approaching Timbuctoo.

On one memorable Thursday afternoon immediately before the long Easter weekend, a family of Hindus came into the office to make arrangements for the funeral for the Saturday and after a few preliminary telephone calls, all was set.

The family had just left the office when the hospital called to tell me that the first doctor could not be found and was on leave for the next two weeks. With the wonderful assistance of the medical records department at the hospital and a friendly doctor, I was able to track the doctor down to his home, where he was packing to leave for holiday. I made arrangement for him to view the deceased and for the second doctor, my own panel doctor, to meet at my chapel so that all forms and formalities could be completed in one go.

I duly removed the deceased from the hospital and awaited the doctors' arrival. The second doctor arrived, my own and we waited and waited. It was early evening by now and obvious that the first doctor was not forthcoming. With a stroke of pure luck, my own doctor not only knew the first but also knew his girlfriend, who was, at that moment, waiting to be collected.

We loaded the remains into our van and, complete with second doctor and required forms, made a mad dash across London to arrive at the girlfriend's house at the same time as the recalcitrant first doctor. The inspection of the body was held in the back of the van in a busy rush hour street in Paddington. He had forgotten!

With a sigh of relief, all the paperwork was assembled and delivered to the crematorium that evening for further inspection before the funeral went ahead without further ado. I often wonder what passersby would have thought if they knew why that van was tearing across London that evening or what those three men were doing climbing in and out of the back of that van in Paddington.

Most doctors are aware of the situation but trouble always seems to occur when the undertaker has been asked to perform the impossible by relatives for one reason or another. It seems as though people who die on the weekends and public holidays are the most nuisance.

For some reason, it would appear that at the weekends death becomes inconvenient, although birth a joyous occasion. We do have to remember that if the coming in outweighed the going out too much, the hospitals would be bursting.

The emergency staffs are geared to work flat out at weekends but it would seem patients on the wards are requested to hang on a little longer. Please remember this for future reference unless the National Health Service goes to a full seven-day service in the meantime.

The Indian funeral goes ahead with the service held at the home in a room cleared for the occasion and, naturally, by their own priest. The mourners nearly always carry the coffin themselves, usually with ten or more bearers and trying to direct these men chattering away in a foreign tongue can be frustrating.

They will, if not stopped, take the coffin and carry it off before the trestles have been set up in the room for the service and can easily try to start off under the coffin facing in different directions, leading to the undertakers staff forcibly turning bearers around to face the correct direction of travel whilst trying to keep a straight face.

Bright robes are placed over the body, oils and powders are anointed, fruits and nuts are placed in the coffin, including coconuts, which can explode in the cremator if they are not cracked beforehand. Every now and then, one gets past the watchful eye of the undertaker and the cremation attendant will remark on this at a later date with tales of woe about the story of the exploding coconut necessitating the complete rebuild of the cremator and the whole cost being borne by the undertaker. These stories abound and, yes, coconuts do sometimes go bang but the damage theories have not been substantiated.

Then to the crematorium with the coffin covered by a beautifully embroidered drape and the committal with more prayers. Now, the immediate family males will witness the cremation. This differs according to crematorium rules, but entails either taking about six mourners behind the scenes where they will push the coffin into the cremator themselves or at the more modern crematorium, they will witness the cremation from a viewing gallery.

The ashes are collected and usually sent to India for dispersal in the river Ganges. It is not a matter of waiting twenty minutes and walking away with an urn, as Hollywood seems to love to portray the event.

Let's explore another myth. I have already explained that the coffin is burnt, complete with handles and fittings and, contrary to popular belief, the ashes received are of the person expected. Cremators can only hold one coffin at a time and usually measure something like seven feet three by two feet six and about two feet high. This excludes some high topped continental coffins but most standard coffins fit.

Before entering the cremator, the nameplate on the coffin is checked and a label fixed to the outside of the cremator. This label will follow the remains though to the 'end'? The cremator now contains coffin, handles, linings and fittings and the dearly beloved.

After the cremation process, the wood and plastic ash have been consumed and with the exception of a few metal staples and screws which will be removed by magnet, all that will be left will be skeleton. The skeleton, being bone, will not burn. Usually, the bones will be ground down to leave what are known as the cremated remains or the new modern term 'Cremains'.

Very often, the Indian families would request that the remains be left ungrounded and provide an urn to hold the bones intact. The longest bone being the thigh bone and the widest, the skull will all fit into a rectangular box about two feet six by ten inches square.

The cremated remains are not only the remains of that person and only that person, but are simply the remains of the bone no matter what anyone may tell you!

Other religions with which we had dealings over the years included both the Plymouth and Strict Brethren, Seventh Day Adventists, Polish, Italian and Czechoslovakian Catholics and Greek Orthodox, to name a few.

Brethren funerals were interesting, as they had no priest. Believing that all men are equal and that no person has the right to preach to another. The service in their hall consists of the members taking their turn to say their own words and relate their own feelings to share with others. The feeling of calm and reverence amongst these people was quite overwhelming.

Funerals for the European Catholics can be quite confusing due to the language barrier. Telephoning in one's own country to find an answer machine in a foreign language and leaving a message in English is a little disconcerting as you are never quite sure whether it will be understood. We always seemed to get through, though.

The Italian church in London is one of the most beautifully decorated I have ever been into, not surprisingly, since the carvings are from the home of sculpture and the home of the Catholic faith itself. However, dealing with an office full of over emotional people, some of whom are crying, some speaking Italian and some trying to communicate some sense of the whole matter to me on the other side of the desk can have its exasperating moments.

From experience, the undertaker is trying to make the arrangements around the normal pattern of a funeral and, of course, there are few differences. To the family, they are the only people who have ever been bereaved and not only can the funeral be lengthy but also making the arrangements.

These arrangements will change many times between the initial contact and the day of the funeral. The number of cars required will change many times, both up and down. The initial plan may be to have the coffin into the church overnight but this may well change if the church is being used that evening for a children's bible class, for example.

Children do not really need to know the stark realities of life at a too early age. The route of the funeral will most certainly change. This can often result in the funeral director realising that there has been talking about a different cemetery and having to point out the error.

However, the most annoying thing is to arrive at the house having planned about twenty minutes to load flowers and cars and family will then decide that they want the coffin in the house for half an hour. This always happens when the rest of the day is very tightly planned, either on behalf of the church, cemetery or undertaker. Arguing with immaculately suited Latin gents on the logistics of planning and timing a funeral with the nagging thought that their violin cases may not be far away is backing a loser from the beginning.

One day, at a Catholic, though not Italian Catholic funeral, we arrived at the house and loaded the flowers and I was trying to load the cars when one of the chief mourners decided that the men were going to walk to the church. There was nothing I could do to change his mind, so off we set, hearse, walking mourners and three limousines empty, apart from the widow and the elderly.

It was about two miles and I led at a brisk pace. The hearse driver, following closely at my heels and chatting to the bearer in the back seat of the hearse, momentarily lost concentration. As I felt the bumper of the hearse touch the back of my boot, horrible thoughts went through my mind as I broke into a quickstep. We arrived at the church shortly after.

Being late at the church was not a problem but I had naturally thought that some of the private cars following were being brought by our group. As the group vacated the roadway, I suddenly realised that all the mourners had walked. After the service, this not unimportant fact dawned on the multitude. There was then much "You stay here whilst I get the car" and "Who has the keys?" followed by portly gents running off in the direction whence we had arrived. The running ceased, soon degenerating into a brisk walk and eventually settling to a more sedate pace and we awaited the return of many cars.

Being late at the cemetery was a problem, especially by nearly an hour. As we had already been into church, the cemetery authority had been told that we would be "committal only" and had allotted us a time of about twenty minutes. This would be ample time. Thirty minutes after our allotted time, arrangements had been made for a West Indian funeral with time allowed for the filling in of the grave as was traditional.

We arrived at the cemetery to see the last limousine of this next funeral entering the gates, followed by many private cars. The grave spaces were both in the same area, the cemetery roads were not wide enough to facilitate two funerals.

I knew that we would have no alternative but to wait. When I tactfully explained that we were the ones who were late and that I had previously pointed these out, frustrations were vented on the fact that the people for whom we were waiting to leave the cemetery were of a different colour.

An ugly scene was averted when pointed out that the public house at the corner of the street was open and might be serving sandwiches. All the men quickly disappeared, followed by some of the ladies.

Fifty minutes or so passed without further incident and the West Indian funeral left the cemetery, followed by the many private cars. Now we had another problem, the public house had indeed served some excellent sandwiches and some excellent ales with which to wash the sandwiches down. Removing the mourners from this establishment took a little longer and, in fact, as we left the cemetery after the committal, it was evident that not all the party had followed into the cemetery.

At about 4 o'clock one Sunday morning, I answered the telephone to be met by a distraught lady speaking in an east European language, none of which made any sense to me at all. Videophones not being commonplace in funeral homes or residences in the east of London, sign language was out of the question.

The next three hours were spent communicating as best we could whilst waiting for an English speaking relative to arrive. During the next few days, I built up an amazing working relationship with the immediate family and friends. Pronouncing the Polish names was certainly an exercise for my tongue whilst remembering the names did the same for my grey matter. Unwittingly, I made such an impression on this close knit community that in later years, calls came from far and wide to my little office in the event of a bereavement.

Apart from the arrangement of funerals within the area, there is also a need for the repatriation of foreign nationals to their own countries and a number of first-generation immigrants to the United Kingdom are sent home for burial. This was quite common to the Caribbean countries from our area, although I have arranged for transportation all over the world. Next time you are travelling on an airliner, consider who might be travelling cargo.

Understandably, there is a copious amount of form filling and regulation for both the country of destination and the carrier and it does take time to learn the ropes but once learnt, the matter is fairly simple for most countries, with some notable exceptions.

The coffin itself has to be metal lined or hermetically sealed. Whilst it is very possible to buy metal liners for coffins and very easy for the larger groups of funeral directors to have these things ready on the shelf, this is not so for the small single shop funeral directors. With limited space and funds, stocking and storing these items for very occasional use is impractical. I decided that it would be possible for me to prepare liners to order for coffins already in stock.

Over the years, this proved a good decision, however it did not take into account the syndrome '253'. The specific number of the syndrome varies from area to area but never along the same bus route. It starts when you stand at a bus stop on a hot sunny day suitably dressed until it rains, making you cold and very wet, at which time six buses arrive all in a line. This may be peculiar to London and is known as bunching. Various attempts have been made over the years to stop this happening, but all have failed since nothing has been able to overcome the fact that the buses themselves like being together.

Syndrome '253' once caused me to have to metal line three coffins in three days, having not done any for months.

Interpretation of the two terms, 'metal lined' and 'hermetically sealed' is interesting in itself since the whole package has to travel freight and is paid for by the kilogram, making repatriation a costly affair.

Some countries insist on metal and this is achieved with zinc sheeting soldered to the shape of the inside of the coffin with wooden rails strung inside to carry the coffin linings. No one would want to see their dearly departed lying in a plan grey zinc liner.

In the later years, I devised a method of lining a coffin with glass reinforced plastic and installing a full length clear acrylic false lid so that the deceased could be viewed at the destination without having to actually unseal the coffin. This method not only gave a much better presentation than the traditional zinc but was also lighter, therefore saving the client money on the freight charges.

The inevitable will always occur at the most inconvenient time and in this, I am no exception. For some incomprehensible reason, when a repatriation is planned, the last person to be consulted is the funeral director, usually late on a Friday afternoon with a request for the impossible before the Monday. It was one such Friday that brought me to line my first coffin in metal.

With all the paperwork ordered and the embalmer on his way, it was not possible to take delivery of the coffin that had been chosen with the required zinc liner in time to catch the flight that we had chosen for the body and relatives to fly on. I located and purchased sufficient zinc sheeting and solder to make the liner and with the metal shears from my tool chest; I set about cutting lining and soldering the coffin.

This first attempt was not only time-consuming but also took a toll on my hands and arms. The sharp cut edges of the zinc sliced into my forearms on many occasions often making the job look like a macabre scene from 'M*A*S*H' and the soldering leaving scorched fingers to contend with.

Task completed, washed clean of my own blood and prepared for its first, last and only inhabitant. The guest of honour embalmed, dressed and placed in residence, the coffin is then either wrapped in hessian or placed in a crate. The latter being more expensive on the freight always prompted me to choose the hessian.

The edges of the coffin had been protected from knock damage, the next task of wrapping takes place with a large needle and twine and finally destination labels and freight information sewn on. Freight must arrive at the airport some four hours before the flight and obviously, the solder sealing and wrapping would take some time to complete and this job was always started in plenty of time. Relatives were therefore informed of the latest possible viewing time to allow this time. The human race, not being perfect, would very seldom let us down and produce a visitor arriving at the time we were about to leave for the airport asking for another quick look.

"I won't take a minute, just one last look?"

Trying to explain that it had just taken me two hours to seal the coffin and prepare it for the flight often seemed beyond their comprehension When one irate family who had been unfortunately delayed in coming to view through an unfortunate mix up with their own flight tickets and discovered that they were unable to view caused me to unload the wrapped coffin from the van and prove to them that they were too late.

This is very distressing as it puts the funeral director in a bad light, however on this occasion the alternative would have been for the coffin to miss the flight by at least two days as the coffin would probably have to be relined after being opened. I was always upset when this sort of thing happened through misfortune or misunderstanding.

Although airlines concur with their regulations for the transportation of human remains, making the job easy and understandable, countries, however, like people, remain stubbornly different. Most undertakers will agree that Italy is the worst country to repatriate a body to, with Turkey following a close second. Ireland, surprisingly, is one of the easiest, with Aer Lingus gaining my vote for the most helpful airline for our job. This may be because of the volume of traffic but they do seem more helpful and understanding.

Once on my way to the airport, the traffic was awful and there was a bad crash on the M4 and I was stuck on the elevated section. With nowhere to go in the foreseeable future, I was pleased to have my portable telephone and called Aer Lingus cargo to let them know my plight. A cheery man with a healthy Irish brogue said not to worry, asked for my number and hung up. I called back to reiterate and was told not to worry, if they couldn't hold the plane any longer, he would call me and the undertaker in Ireland. How's that for service?

There were, of course, some disasters, none of which were attributable to me, I am glad to say. Notably, one was when a young girl had died and was being sent home to one of the small Caribbean islands. Firstly, the mother and father were very nice people and were handling their tragic bereavement well. I did my very best to make everything go so smoothly for them and received smiles and tearful gratitude for my efforts. I had paid the freight fully from my end through one of the major carriers and expected no problems.

Late into the night, I received a telephone call from the irate father. The coffin had not arrived and was still in Miami. The father then had to fly back to Miami and pay cash for the onward flight. I did manage to obtain a refund for the gentleman, but I never received a letter of apology, nor did the customer.

--

Chapter Five
Breakdowns

Breakdowns are the worst thing that can happen at a funeral but as the saying goes, 'Effluent Occurs' and they have to be overcome. The hearse has a fifty-fifty chance of causing problems, whereas the limousine is almost fully guaranteed to annoy. The reason the hearse gets away with it is that the interested party has a one-way ticket. Funnily enough, this is the reason for the whole occasion.

Attitudes of the public differ tremendously towards these unfortunate events, from the understanding, "Well, these things happen and dad would have liked to be late for his funeral, wouldn't we all!"

To the other extreme of "Do we have to get out of the car whilst you change the wheel?"

This on a twenty-year-old car fitted with its own hydraulic jacks when the driver is praying that they will work just once more.

Maintenance is a way of reducing the probability of silly breakdowns, making the driver push is the way of ensuring the car has enough petrol before leaving the garage. Part failures and punctures are mostly beyond care.

When the limousine pulls up to the house behind the hearse, the driver cannot always see the empty glass bottle in the gutter. If the conductor has not seen this and removed it from harm's way, a resounding 'POP' will alert one's ears to the now unavoidable danger. The staff will then all gather round to await the dreaded 'PSSSST!'

The tyres on all these beasts are sturdy and more often than not, they make it through without getting pssst. The driver should then clear the glass to avoid further possibility of puncture but there is always that nagging doubt on the way that a sliver of glass is lodged in the tyre. One day we thought we had escaped tyre damage after our bottle had burst but as we were loading the flowers, there was a little pop and a pssst and the limousine driver said, "Oh Luck!" I think.

The psst continued as the big black beast creaked and settled slowly but surely down into the gutter with various staff scurrying about for a jack before it settled fully down. The camber was too steep to risk the use of the car's own jacks. They would have surely jacked the car up far enough so that they would have bent, thereby leaving the car stranded in mid-air. This time we were lucky and the spare wheel had air in it. The only casualty was a sore finger and a dirty shirt cuff.

The first breakdown of the hearse I experienced was luckily on the way back from Enfield Crematorium, I was driving the limousine with the conductor and we left the cemetery gates to see our hearse parked in a bus stop, driver standing next to it holding something in his hand. I knew he had not run out of petrol as we had filled up that morning. It was unlikely that it was dirty petrol because it would have shown up sooner. So, what in the world would make a Rolls Royce stop after only forty-two years?

As we approached, I recognised the item in the driver's hand as the gear lever. Of all the places it could have broken, it was in neutral; I wondered whether it was still under warranty as we came to a halt.

Now I was the limousine driver and he was the hearse driver, so why, five minutes later was I left standing by the side of an inoperative vehicle with a small adjustable spanner, a screwdriver and a small box containing what looked more like scrap metal than a toolkit. One thing that struck me as odd was that the sun was out.

The Rolls Royce 25/30HP is an interesting beast as was the following model in that it had (or had had); its gear lever on the right-hand side of the driver connected under the floorboards by an enclosed shaft to the gearbox itself. This putting the gear lever and incidentally the handbrake too, right in your way as you enter the car.

The later model had an interesting quirk as the gear lever was a little shorter and angled further back towards the driver. The lever could quite easily find its way up your trouser leg as you entered the car, once sat in the car, it was impossible to lift your leg off the lever without leaving the car. Seeing a driver get into a car, wait until it was time to go and then get out, only to get straight back in again and drive off caused some odd looks to all who had not driven a car like it.

Back to the job in hand, I started to remove the floorboards of the "shiftless" creature to find out what could be done. The lever had broken at its weakest point where it was joined to the shaft. I tried to coax the shaft into selecting any gear for the trip home but with all the odd shaped spanners and shafts available, I had no joy even though the gearbox itself was silky smooth.

Another hearse pulled up. "Are you alright?"

"Having a wonderful time, old chap!" I replied with floorboards up and hands covered in red hot oil.

"You're Bob's son, aren't you?"

"No!"

"Sorry we can't stop we've got another job on. Good luck!" and off they went.

A friendly, helpful crowd are undertakers. An RAC man stopped and walked around to the nearside, removed his hat, scratched his head. "Are you alright?"

"Having a wonderful time, old chap!" I couldn't resist it.

"You don't see many of these!"

"What do you mean, there is a crematorium just here, you get hearses up and down here all day."

"No, I mean Rolls Royce."

"Oh, really."

"I've never seen one this old on the road before." He was, even then, good enough to have a look at the problem. After further removal of hat and scratching of head, he asked "Are you members?"

We were not, so this was a good cue for an exit.

"Good luck."

I managed to remove the covering plates from the gear lever housing in an effort to get closer to the point of breakage and hopefully make a temporary fix to drive home. I arrived at the stage of having removed lots of little pieces and some large ones too, to realise that I was going to get precisely nowhere. I decided to attack the job from the other end.

After removing a few more floorboards, I noticed an inspection plate on the top of the gearbox itself, which to my surprise, not only came off easily but also revealed the gear selecting mechanism. With the aid of a rod, bar, pinch or pole, I simply selected third gear.

I could have now driven home after replacing the floorboards had I not started at the wrong end. So I had to replace all the little bits and the large ones.

With no bits left to put back, except those that one hopes wouldn't really matter, I drove off. The engine being huge and designed to take any amount of driving up and down mountains and all across the world on basically unmade roads and at what are now considered suicidal speeds; I took the vehicle from stand still in third gear with much more ease than I had expected. I drove back to the garage. The next task was to repair the vehicle for the following day's work.

I made a few telephone calls. "Have you got a gear lever for a 1936 Rolls Royce 25/30 in chrome?"

I couldn't actually find anyone who could understand my request and decided that they were all watching the same Marx brother's film. I set about a repair.

I removed the broken piece of lever which entailed taking off the lots of little pieces and the big bits too, together with a whole lot more and welded up a temporary repair. This lasted the next three years until we sold the vehicle. After I reassembled, I did not have any big bits left and only a few little bits and it all worked.

There were three other memorable hearse breakdowns in which I was involved, the next chronologically was when my mother's father's brother's son's wife's sister's husband or 'Uncle Bob' was still managing when we had replaced the Royce's with newer Vanden Plas cars whilst I renovated the former.

One very hot day, travelling to Manor Park Cemetery very slowly with three limousines, taking the long route to waste time, the brakes on one of the front wheels decided to stick on. It must be remembered that these vehicles were designed just after the Second World War and such occurrences were virtually commonplace compared to the far safer cars designed today.

With the car travelling so slowly, being black and absorbing heat, the brakes binding and requiring more power to push the vehicle along, overheating problems were my main worry and I was trying to ignore the smoke rising from the seizing brake drum, the delinquent wheel was the front right so impossible to miss either the sight or the smell of the smoke.

Helpful passersby were falling over each other to inform us "Hey, look, your wheel's on fire!" all waving and shouting whilst I was trying to act nonchalant, breaking all the rules of my atheism and requesting assistance.

Half way down the The Whipps Cross Road I decided that either I was right or "He" had thought it an inopportune moment to grant salvation or maybe it was something to do with the guy lying by my left ear. The hearse succumbed to the heat and came to rest. We sat there. We had plenty of water and there were no leaks. What had happened was that the fuel was evaporating in the heat before reaching the carburettor? I thought that a few minutes wait and liberal sloshing of water over the fuel system might be sufficient cooling to reach the cemetery.

A face peered from a passing car. "Having trouble?"

I bit my lip and looked up and there was dear old Bert Higgins. "I'll get my hearse back in five minutes!"

I said thank you to more than one person, just in case. This was one of the nicest things about the East End funeral trade and one of the first things I taught my own drivers was to help whenever they could in such situations.

Bert arrived, we transferred coffin, flowers and off they went, leaving "guess who" with the very large hot black uncooperative proverbial baby! It was not long before the whole thing cooled sufficiently to be driven home at normal speeds, the additional wind flow providing enough cooling. That evening I managed to fix the brakes and later fitted an auxiliary electric fuel pump in case of similar problems in the future heatwaves. Winter promptly set in!

The next occasion of hearse failure was during the conducting of my very first funeral, that of a very young child, where the coffin was going into the house for the morning and we were collecting later that afternoon. First thing Monday morning, how could I ever forget it. The battery of the hearse was flat, now, a four litre six-cylinder engine and a heavy thing to start by hand. We had no choice and left it running for the next hour while it was washed and until we arrived at the house.

"Now, Frank, don't, whatever you do, switch it off!"

We stopped outside the house and as he got out of the car, his left hand went over to the key and—silence.

"Too late now. Let's get on with the job!"

So we took the little coffin into the house and left the little girl there with family and relatives, came outside to our electrical flat. After a considerable amount of handle swinging, muttering and swearing, it started and we drive back, my growling at poor old Frank slowly abated. A hearse hired for the afternoon and new batteries fitted in our hearse, we were all ready for the next day.

The final time was with the Silver Cloud, it had started to use water, so I had pressurised the system in a hope of finding the leak. Finding all good, we went out on to work the following week. We were outside the church when I decided to check the oil. To my horror, I found water in the oil. Again, I was lucky to be able to hire a hearse from a local funeral director at short notice. Another job to fix the hearse.

The only other time when the hearse was damaged was on the way back from the City of London Crematorium when our Eddie was driving and waiting at a roundabout to turn right. A large box van came by on his left-hand side, whilst taking the sharp left turn, the tail swing sliced into the rear nearside wing, causing extensive damage. The following dialogue was reported as follows.

"Sorry, Guv, my fault," said the van driver.

"Gawd luv a duck, not only do you 'av to 'it an 'earse, you 'av to pick a bloody Rolls Royce," his mate added.

The haulage company were very good after the initial shock of my telephone call and the repairs were carried out promptly. The unfortunate cost of hiring a hearse for the interim period was eventually borne by the insurance after a few sharp intakes of breath.

What can you say when your hearse is charged by a bullock and damaged extensively? I would have liked to have seen the expression on the claims officer's face. The hearse, a Ford and grey in colour, was travelling along the same Whipps Cross Road complete with coffin, flowers and limousines full of mourners. I should mention that this road is part of Epping Forest and one of the few roads I know where the cows grazing have more rights than people. Cows usually herd and will tend to follow the leader, even across roads.

Many people in the area well know the wait whilst cows meander around the road, oblivious to the frustration of the rush hour travellers. The driver of the hearse had waited long enough and thought his best plan of action was to edge forward and try to push his way gently through the herd, he was apparently doing well until one young bullock decided on his right of way. I can imagine the horror on the faces of most of the occupants as the bullock not only kicked in one side wing of the hearse but then charged the other side with a good headbutt. The question on most of the trade's lips was of immediate concern.

"Was it hurt?"

"No, they were all fine and drove to the cemetery."

"Not the lads, you fool, the bullock!"

A quick breakdown story for the Rolls Royce Phantom was when uncle Bob was driving it and kept slowing down, never going over about twelve miles per hour. I stopped the hearse; the limousine pulled up behind us, third and fourth gears had failed. This being a day when we were late and going to a crematorium on the outskirts of London. I remembered from the manual that it was not possible to exceed fifty-six miles per hour in second gear. That would do, so I selected 'Fixed Second Gear' on the gear lever. The car went through the entire funeral in that gear and nobody even noticed.

When a limousine breaks down, the signal used to be to switch on headlights, this would be followed through by all the other cars until, with any luck, the hearse driver would notice and stop. Today it seems popular for all funeral vehicles to drive around with their lights on. In times gone by, this would mean they would never move.

All drivers remain with their cars and the conductor walks back to the lame duck. It can be quite a walk if the message has taken some time to reach the front of the cortege. Then, if it is not possible to fix the problem in a few minutes, transfer passengers to other limousines and private cars, leaving the lone driver to fend for himself. When the sole limousine breaks down, if the local undertaker is on speaking terms and can help you are in luck, otherwise you grab as many taxis as will do the job offering vast rewards.

A notable crash of funeral vehicles happened on the Great Cambridge Road with hearse and three limousines. Luckily, I had nothing to do with the funeral or the cars. Travelling close together and at a reasonable speed on the dual carriageway, the traffic lights changed to red and the hearse stopped, the first limousine failed to stop or to put it more accurately, failed to stop before the bumper of the hearse, similarly, the second limousine failed to stop. The third limousine driver, being more alert, brought his vehicle to a safe stop without damage.

Unfortunately, the car behind him had not taken so much notice of the road ahead and ploughed into the last limousine, shunting it firmly into the rear of the one in front. Mirth spread throughout the rest of the trade for many a day.

Chapter Six
The Public Mortuary

The term itself is enough to make most people's knees wobble, but as mentioned earlier, it is a necessary part of our society in the prevention of disposing of evidence of crimes. Without going into any detail and in general, if a person has not seen a doctor within the past fourteen days and died, it is usually unexpected and the cause of death has to be investigated.

The person responsible for this is the coroner. This man, often both a brilliant doctor and lawyer, as with Dr Chambers in our area, wields a great deal of power and respect. He is assisted by the coroner's officer(s) who are police constables. Some PCs like the job, some don't. Our little mob in Hackney were friendly, fun and helpful. Once I had built up a good rapport and professional relationship with these constables, they not only became good friends but were also invaluable at times when I wanted to perform the odd miracle for a client.

The technicians who perform the postmortems vary from friendly souls who are happy to see a smiling face at any time, to the grumpy creatures that leave the undertakers happy to see a dead face. This analogy goes for hospital mortuary attendants too. Either, of course, can make the undertakers job easy or downright impossible, most sensible staff treat these beings with a good amount of respect.

There are some who take their job and the regulations too far and my Bête Noir was at an internationally famous hospital in Central London. This man had a lunch break of about two hours and over the years, I do not think I managed to effect one removal with ease, I was once told that the coffin was too large. This person almost brought me and my staff to physical violence on more than one occasion. Sending a new man there was always an event to be thoroughly prepared. for. "Now Phil, you're going to this hospital and here is how you find the mortuary, here is the paperwork and here is the coffin. Be nice to Len and make sure you get there before twelve because he won't let you in otherwise," was the usual sort of instruction and immediately prompted the reply, "What is this guy, some sort of God?"

"For today, yes and don't get upset with him!"

"I can't see any problem; I am just going to collect a body from a hospital, aren't I? So why all the fuss?" asked Phil.

"No fuss, he can just be very strict about the rules, that is all."

"This guy is just a mortuary attendant, right?"

"Yes, but you must be back for the funeral at one thirty, OK?"

And off they would go, small bets would be placed amongst the old hands as to whether the removal would be affected first time out and without aggravation. We awaited their return with bated breath.

After a considerable amount of time, the door crashed open, the one who had wagered "No and return after an argument" would put their hand out for the booty.

"That man's an idiot!" shout Phil.

"Listen, in God's truth, I got there at quarter to twelve right, quarter to and I'm ringing the bell, on my life."

"That won't be necessary Phil, have a cup of tea before we go out on the funeral."

"Ta. So I'm ringing this bell, right and through the little window, I see the bloke pushing a trolley through these doors and I'm hammerin' on the door in case the bell doesn't work," he continued.

"Yes Phil, sit down and have a rest, keep your voice down, there are people in the office."

"I know he saw me standing there. Then I see this phone on the wall and it says, 'If no reply call this number' and I get this soppy cow who says he's in the bl**&! mortuary and I tell her, I know that but 'e won't bl**&! well answer. I tell her, on my life."

"Anyway, I'm ringing the bell and 'ammerin the door an 'e comes out at three minutes past and says 'ees off t' lunch, well I tried t' remain calm 'cos it makes us look bad, well I told 'im I wanted this body now and I'd been 'ammering 'n' all."

"Did you get the body?" I asked.

"Yes," the wager changes hands, "eventually. I wasn't gonna leave it there an' 'ave t' go all up there again, was I."

Old hands are suitably impressed and the 'rookie' status is replaced with 'minor deity'. I never did ask how the miracle was achieved but the police never arrived and there were no headlines in the paper so I assume the attendant survived.

The postmortem room is an awe-inspiring place with its seven-foot porcelain or stainless steel tables and drains running everywhere, sinks and cabinets containing shiny carpentry like tools. When all tables are vacant and the room spotless it looks pretty grim to a new lad, but when filled with corpses in 'kit form' and bowls full of various organs accompanied by the unavoidable and unmistakable smell, it can create sometimes more than a lasting impression on the unaware rookie.

At Hackney, as one enters the refrigerator room, the PM room is situated through a clear door on the left as you enter. Many times, I have gone through the warning.

"Now as we go through this door, there is a glass door on your left, just ignore it for now and I'll take you in there after we are loaded up." I don't mind carrying the guy to the van whilst unconscious but he could help load up first.

"Now just look straight ahead."

Too late, there must be some sort of eyeball magnet in these places. The Adam's apple shifts up and down with a little 'GULP', nostrils quiver, washes of mid to lower spectrum colour invade the face, knees shake.

"You're alright, son, you'll get used to it." Some do, some don't.

There are worse sights in store for the rookie and with any luck, they will come by slowly and not all on the first day, as with my own initiation.

The postmortem itself is a matter of opening up the entire body cavity from neck to pelvis and investigation of the organs is made, furthermore, the brain is removed from the cranium and inspection carried out, then the whole lot is sewed back together. Not a pretty sight or smell, especially with a 'full house'. A squeaky radio often sits on a windowsill announcing today's news and weather, making the whole scene even more bizarre.

Occasionally in a busy postmortem room, an embalmer can be spotted, usually suited and singing or whistling to himself as he pumps, massages, prods, sews and creates what can only be described as the veritable silk purse from the sow's ear.

Embalming or Preservative Treatment, as it is popularly called nowadays. Why do we have to change the names of things? Do we fool anyone? The Undertaker became the Funeral Director; I suppose the Embalmer will become the Beautician, which will upset some, with the dustman becoming the Refuse Disposal Operatives, the Funeral Director must, at some time, become the Human Disposal Consultant.

Preservative treatment is a very good thing as it not only restores the features of the body and face to a less morbid look, but also sanitises, protecting staff and family from possible infections.

People's attitude to this varies from "No, we don't want them to be prodded or pulled about anymore." To "Well, if we have her embalmed, how long will she last?"

"Well, sir, it will not make the slightest difference since we have just made arrangements to set fire to her at midday on Thursday!"

The process itself is a matter of finding or "raising" a fairly major artery at one point in the body and injecting fluid that will push out the darker venal blood from the system and remove any clots or bruising. The fluid itself disinfects and also has the property of drying the skin, giving the advantage of less condensation and ease of taking makeup.

I had fought shy of watching the process for many years since I am the world's best patient when it comes to any sort of injection. I faint, giving doctors an easy target, however, as I was so impressed by the results that could be achieved, my professional curiosity eventually got the better of me.

One day, Frank, a previous employee and now a full-time embalmer, was due to arrive in the evening. I prepared myself for watching and learning. He already knew of my plans and when he arrived, we had the usual cup of tea, everything revolved around tea at Mosses and we used to use about a pound of tea a week among three permanent full-time staff and visitors. I had the body prepared on the embalming table in the workshops, as usual.

"You ready?" said Frank, getting up, a smile on his face.

"As I'll ever be," I replied as we made our way from the back office. I had by now been in the trade for some considerable number of years, I had seen, picked up and disposed of some pretty grisly sights. I had been in rooms where embalmers were working and always managed to look the other way. This time was different, I was going to watch the whole thing from beginning to end. I was standing next to a man with whom I worked for many years and he was merely going to show me how to embalm a body, I had nothing to worry about, except the lump in my throat and sweating of my palms.

The gleaming tools from the folding case took on a more sinister meaning than before, as they were laid out in preparation for use.

"You all right?" said Frank.

"Yes," I sweated as he brandished the scalpel. I looked away as the blade neared the neck.

"You're not watching!" noticed Frank.

"Well, maybe I'll just miss the first cut."

"Coward."

"You guessed."

"What are the lads going to say when I tell them that their guvner is afraid of watching a little embalming," jibed Frank.

"What is Frank going to do when I get the air drill out?"

Frank, I knew from old and has a morbid fear of dentists and the sound of my little air drill whirring away always struck untold fear into his mind. Know your friends very well if you are going to let them know your own fears.

We progressed. Once the first cut was over, a very small incision just above the inner end of the right collarbone, the gentle parting of the muscle and raising the artery, was quite fascinating. The artery is opened and the injector inserted, the fluid is pumped around the body. The first direction is downward from the carotid and you can actually follow the flow firstly through right arm to the hand, then right and left legs, on to the left arm and finally to the left-hand side of the face.

Following this flow around, the body is accompanied by massage to assist the break-up of the darker venal blood, the result is an amazing change from the deathly pallor we started with to a much pinker and more natural look of slumber. The injector is then turned to face upward, this will complete the process to the right-hand side of the face.

We have now forced all the blood from the arteries, capillaries and veins into the central body cavity, about four or five pints of pink fluid have been used. What goes in must come out and this takes a little getting used to, a pipe is inserted into one of the chambers of the heart and the venal blood is drawn out, not a pleasant sight. Additional stronger fluid is then spread about the cavity through the same hole.

Now finished with the gruesome bit, it is a matter of tying off the artery and sewing up the holes, a quick invisible mend to hold the jaw in place with dentures fitted by which time the texture of the skin has changed from a damp feeling of death to a dryer and softer feel altogether. Eyes closed, makeup applied, leaving just a comb through the hair to finish the job.

"How's that?" asked Frank. I had been watching when I wanted to and not when I didn't.

"Well, I didn't fall over, did I?"

"The next one will be easier, you will soon get used to it, anyway you were the person who taught me to stitch up a mouth!"

"That's different."

"No, it isn't." He was right about that.

We went through the same thing another few times over the next few weeks and I began to get more used to the process but steadfastly refused to watch him work on a postmortem case. This is one of the good things about being the boss.

With mixed blessings, my great day came. The usual situation had arisen, late in the afternoon on the Friday preceding a bank holiday, unable to get an embalmer before the Tuesday, a body in desperate need of treatment and with relatives wanting to view on the Saturday morning. I had no choice but to do the job myself—GULP!

I had all the right tools, I had all the right fluids, I had cotton wool, I had the gloves, I had the body. I had no excuse to delay the event any longer but I was still doing my best.

There I stood, scalpel in hand, delaying the time, hoping the phone would ring, anything. My hand moved closer and back again, this happened many times until eventually I thought I had better go to the loo—and back to the scalpel.

At last, the first incision was made, it didn't hurt and I was still standing. The search for the artery began. Sometime later, I had convinced myself that I was dealing with some sort of freak without the usual cardiovascular system. I extended the incision and looked again. This continued, I began to sweat, "It must be here, somewhere."

When Frank had done it, there it was staring at you, trust me to start with a duff dead. To my great relief, I found something and pulled it up, "Aha," feeling very proud of myself, I prepared the injector.

At this time for some unknown reason, my nose began to itch uncontrollably, I tried twitching it, I tried rubbing it against my shoulder, which made it worse,

I tried breathing strangely and I tried blowing at it. There was only one thing that would do it and that was a good scratch.

Scratching is a totally natural thing to do and most of the time, the average human being will do this quite unconsciously, I had just found an occasion when natural reactions take second place. I used the natural break and had a cup of tea.

Back to it, approaching the job anew and refreshed, it looked less daunting although the incision was quite a lot larger than the neat three-quarter inch jobs that Frank had performed, I was thankful that we could hide this under a high collar. The injection process complete, I then came to the pump out. This entailed making another surgical entry and further delays whilst I adjusted my nerve. I found the correct place with my fingers and presented the instrument, I steeled my nerve and found that I had done it, everything went as it should. The job was now over apart from the sewing up, I felt very proud of myself. Furthermore, there were no leaks or mishaps before the funeral.

To some people this may seem distasteful, however, when you think what doctors do to the living, it puts a different light on the subject.

I did, after some time, learn how to deal with postmortem cases, the details of which I will not go into. Over the years, I became proficient at embalming and appreciated the presentation improvements that I could achieve. In hindsight, with apologies to my earlier efforts.

The complimentary art to embalming is the makeup and finding this most interesting, I bought a specialist makeup kit and learnt how to use that. Mostly, the making up of a body was a quite simple matter of a little powder and rouge. An over made-up face can look awful. There were the occasions when virtual plastic surgery was required and this is where the kit really proved its worth.

I had experimented with the makeup and its use when I had time using the kit's creams, fillers and colourings on various cases to blend out marks and scars whilst trying to maintain a natural look. Many times I would create what I thought to be the desired effect and, after standing back to have a look, decide it looked awful, take it all off and start again. Sometimes, I would get so engrossed in trying to perfect the art that I would end up spending two or three hours on one person without realising the passage of time.

On the majority of occasions, the hard work involved in makeup would go completely unnoticed. This is the way it should be, as with any repair job to anything, it should be invisible and therefore unremarkable.

On very few occasions did we know beyond doubt that we had done the job right, many times, relatives would politely say how nice they thought the result was, leaving that uncertainty in my mind that I had put on either too much, too little or the wrong colour makeup. When most relatives view the loved ones, makeup is superfluous and they are there to pay their last respects to a memory but feel they should be near the remains to do so.

There is a natural fear of the dead so the mind shuts out the physical, therefore as long as the thing in the box bears some resemblance to the memory, the mind is satisfied. It is important that eyes and mouth are closed and the mask it not grotesque, hence the importance of the right amount of makeup. The balance is a very fine line.

Children have a different view of everything, black and white, right and wrong. This realisation was once brought home to me very firmly. An elderly lady had been knocked down by a large truck and her face had required many stitches in the emergency theatre. She had died a day or so later. I had accepted arrangements for the funeral, knowing that they all wanted to view the body and the fact that she had been in a road accident but not knowing the extent of her facial injuries.

After the postmortem, I was presented with quite a job on my hands. I started, of course, with the normal embalming after a postmortem examination. This takes some time longer than normal cases, this time even more so, in view of the accident before death. This complete, I was left with the face to work on. Before starting work on this, I decided to leave the embalming process to settle and continue its drying until that evening.

I remember starting work at about five thirty after the lads had gone home and I had dinner booked for nine at a local restaurant. The first part of the rebuild was to remove the stitches and stick the skin together and make the job as flat as possible, this is rather like matching wallpaper, cheap wallpaper that stretches, made more difficult by the glue being rather like superglue in that it does not give you a second chance.

This was accomplished, to my great surprise and with the greatest amounts of luck, first time, I really thought I had the job on the run. We then came to the filling step, to hide the mark which ran over the eye, it would be necessary to add a small amount of the correct colour to the filler. There are a myriad of shades to mix with the wax filler so with much consulting the instruction book for blending the colours, a great deal of time was consumed.

The instructions stated that blending was to be done at body temperature, this posed a dilemma as within the workshop area we had two very different 'body temperatures'. I managed to guess right the first time.

Since I was, of course, wearing rubber gloves, finding something at the required 98.5 degrees was more difficult than for a baker or nursery attendant who might be expected to provide the same on occasions. Initially, this was achieved by rolling back the 'marigolds' and using the palm of my left hand but this proved to be awkward when wanting to use the fingers so as time went on I discarded the left glove, soon to be followed by the right.

This may at first sight seem a foolhardy thing to do whilst dealing with the dead, however, very few people die of contagious diseases when they do, we are usually informed and anyway, I had just gone through the process of injecting the body with a formalin solution strong enough to frighten the hell out of any bacteria or disease, self-respecting or not.

A mix of filler putty that looks a perfect match when offered up to the skin on the tiny mixing trowel looks quite different when applied and it was a matter of putting on and removing it for further blending, many many times. Problems always seemed to occur when the addition of the minutest amount of colour would change the shade far beyond the subtlety required. Eventually, I achieved a colour that would blend in with a dusting of powder.

Now we had a surface of the tiniest amount of filler over the cracks blending out to the skin on either side. Having been applied with the trowel, the surface was flat and totally unlike flesh. The lines and wrinkles have to be applied. With the tiny trowel, the forehead lines are raked in, just enough to look like a line but not enough to reveal the damage below.

It was at about this time that I realised that one of the eyebrows had been completely removed. I stole some hair from the back of the head and proceeded to stick on eyebrows. People have a great number of eyebrows. This done and it still didn't look right and then it dawned on me, there were no pores on the filler. I was dreading the painstaking application of the little dots when it dawned on me to use one of the makeup brushes as a pore producer, this worked well and produced a pleasing result.

The final application of makeup was now a simple job until the dusting out of face powder with brush successfully removed or ruined lines and pores, which had to be replaced after the powdering.

I was congratulating myself on a job well done when the phone rang. I had switched the telephone over to the mobile number to save me from running back and forth to the office every time I had a call.

"Where the hell are you? You were supposed to pick me up at eight! I suppose you're in a pub chatting up some woman." The girlfriend.

"Wrong about the pub, there is a woman, but she is being neither talkative nor cooperative." She did have a point; it was ten to nine. I covered the body, washed, changed and went to dinner on my knees.

"What's that on your hand?"

"Makeup!" I said, knowing instinctively how to appease the situation. Some of the colouring had marked my skin and it had not come off with a scrub.

"So you let the women kiss your hand now, do you?"

"Look, luv, if I could spell sarcastic, I'd be a writer, now shut it." I let her buy me dinner out of the kindness of my heart.

The next day, we carefully placed the body in the coffin, all went well and I managed to keep prying fingers from the "where was that scar, you can't even see where it was." And the "Was it this side or that side?" enquiries.

The relatives came and viewed expressing much pleasure and admiration, however, it was the statement of one young boy that gave me the most pleasure.

"That's not my Gran. She's got stitches all over her face!"

There was much coming and going to visit the old lady and before we put the lid on the coffin, we noticed that someone had been unable to resist a prod at my handiwork.

Over the years, there was only one time that caused me to miss a heartbeat, other than the early days. I was in a hurry, as usual and the body that had to be embalmed was a postmortem case, therefore requiring more time. I was working with a very small injector, a clamp and a scalpel, all of which were in my hands at the same time.

I had the clamp and injector in my left hand and scalpel in my right. The scalpel slipped from my hand and was descending, point first, towards my left hand, as I sharply moved my left hand out of the way of the falling instrument, the scalpel, caught in the rubber of the glove of the upward moving hand.

The result was the business end of the scalpel, ran across the palm of my right hand, leaving the glove cut open from the base of the index finger to the diagonally opposite point of my palm and past my wrist until it stopped at the sleeve of my coat. I waited for the blood to flow, mine, but on further inspection, there was not even a mark to my skin although the glove itself was history. A good way of checking for small cuts was a liberal dowsing with embalming fluid. If there was a cut, it would sting like hell, but also kill anything nasty in the cut. I do not think the Institute of Embalmers would recommend this practice.

Chapter Seven
Nuts

A funeral needs many things to have any chance of success. The basic requirement of a body is often the least of our worries, if you wait long enough, one will always turn up.

Whilst it is quite possible for the same person to make the arrangements, collect the body, embalm it, prepare the coffin, display the body in the coffin, wash and service the cars and with the help of trolleys etc. make the funeral happen at the crematorium, there is one thing that he cannot do without. The 'nut' behind the wheel.

Every car you have that you intend to put on the road must have a driver. This driver must also be trained as a funeral driver. The average Ford Escort driver would have kittens just climbing up to sit in the front of one of the larger funeral cars. The 'Nut' is not only your greatest asset but also your biggest liability.

Two months before 'uncle' Bob retired, our old hearse driver, Tom, also retires so that I was left to employ all my own staff. I had a clear start which I felt was an advantage, bad habits could not permeate and the job would be done my way. I hoped.

A young man had started with the firm when Tom had left and he seemed to be getting on well enough. When the time was approaching for Bob to retire, he had asked for two weeks off as he had some business to sort out and knew that in September, I would need him. Since he had not returned to work, nor contacted us, the week before Bob was due to finish, I was concerned about being left without any staff.

I had not been able to contact the man, by luck, I was introduced to a local guy, Frank, who had previous experience of the trade which I viewed with mixed feelings, however, just nine weeks before, he had been in hospital for an operation to fuse three of his vertebrae following a back injury the previous year. I thought I could not really take this man seriously in view of his injuries and the responsibility that the company would be taking on regarding his future health. We met one afternoon as I was about to leave for the local hospital on a removal. He asked where I was going and if he could come along. He had been told to take things easy but pronounce fit by his doctor.

We were both very concerned when it came to the lifting, as well as being pleasantly surprised. Although he said that it felt a little stiff, there was no pain. We went back to the shop and he helped for the remainder of the day. His experience with the trade had been with driving only and I had to introduce him to the coffin fitting experiences with all the joys of hammers and thumbs to look forward to.

As far as I could see so far, Frank had three attributes, he was a good driver, a willing worker and a damned nice guy.

"When can you start?" I asked.

"I hoped I already had." He did.

Initially, I kept him on the fairly light jobs until we knew the strain he could take and to give him time to ease his muscles back into lifting, luckily for us both, all went well and as long as there were no shocks, any weight was fine. At this time, I was being very careful with my shoulder having been into hospital myself earlier that year to have glass removed from my shoulder following my injury nearly four years before, so I started with a right pair of invalids. I never did see the other man at work.

Uncle Bob still came in to help on a part time basis and so did his wife Winnie until I had found my first receptionist, which happened to be Frank's wife.

Advertisements with the job centre always took a long time to produce anything, even if at all. This is quite understandable if you think about the scene. A guy is unemployed and has limited qualifications so he goes to the job centre and looks at the cards. Amongst the 'Drivers' section is a card that is titled 'Funeral Assistant'. Now can you imagine what pictures this might conjure up in the mind of an ex delivery driver?

Shakespeare started the rot when he dragged poor old Yorik back from his final resting place to play a scene that he couldn't interest any of his contemporary actors in playing. Hollywood wouldn't leave Count Dracula in Transylvania in peace, Christopher Lee had put paid to the idea that anyone could ever die a normal death and what with 'Dad's Army' showing the undertaker as being a Scottish weirdo constantly proclaiming that we were all doomed, the queue for jobs outside my front door consisted of a long line of blank spaces.

A young man eventually braved his way through the sea of ghoulish impressions, made an appointment, crept nervously up to my door in broad daylight and rang the bell. From where I stood, he was quite normal, early twenties, average height, slim build, blond hair that needed a cut, I opened the door. I should mention that our shop door, like many other shop doors, remained unlocked during business hours and the act of opening the door would ring a bell, simple but effective, the idea has been in use for decades.

However, for many, the idea of actually going in would be more than their media induced fear could handle. Over the years, I forgot to lock the shop door at night on many occasions, nobody ever came in when the lights were out.

"Hello, you must be John. Do come in." From his point of view, there, standing inside this shop, was a fair-haired man of about thirty wearing an ordinary suit and smiling. He glanced quickly around to make sure that he hadn't come to the wrong place. Well, it looked like an undertakers, so who was this perfectly ordinary looking man standing there, where was the top hat, the hooked nose, the ashen face and crooked smile. The bottom jaw quivered and the Adam's apple rose and fell.

"Mm Mr Moss?" he stammered.

"Yes, come in, you're in good time, go into the office, sit down." I closed the door behind him as I waved and smiled at an acquaintance passing by. As John made his way into the office, every cell in his body was telling him that something was wrong. He sat bolt upright and so close to the edge of the chair that it nearly tipped forward. He leant dangerously forward and handed me his interview card from the job centre.

"Er, I er was er—"

"Expecting someone much older with dyed black hair, ash white face, wearing a full mourning dress and looking positively dead," I butted in.

"Er, well, I, er, suppose so," he said, a broad grin swept across his face in response to my smile.

"I'm trying to start a rumour that undertakers are real human beings in their spare time. Smoke?" He obviously did, by the colour of his fingers. I asked him to tell me what he had been doing since he had left school, as I lit his cigarette and took one myself.

"I didn't think you were supposed to smoke at interviews." He was beginning to relax.

"Well, I am looking for a driver and somebody to train to be useful to me and you, are looking for a job so, if we have a discussion about it and then put our cigarettes out and have an interview, will that do?" I said with a smile. "So tell me about yourself."

He started and we began to chat. He asked about the job and what it would entail, I expressed the need for quiet formality when customers were present and stressed the friendly atmosphere that I wanted as a work environment. He was fairly relaxed by now and I had virtually decided to give him a job pending a "driving test". Frank returned from a removal and his face appeared at the textured glass door to check whether I was with anyone before coming into the main office. John noticed this face at the window.

"Come in Frank!" I called.

"This is the black-haired old man with a white face and a hooked nose you were expecting when you arrived," I told John.

"I'm Frank." He strode across the room to shake John's hand, "Tea time Boss?"

"Milk and sugar. John, don't be frightened of him," he indicated in my direction, "He's an ogre all week but he cries on paydays!" and left the room.

With all his illusions of an undertaker totally shattered, I took young John out and showed him the chapel, workshops and garage, I told him not to be frightened of the size of the cars and that he would have plenty of time to get used to them before going out on the work. We joined Frank in the second office for tea.

"Are there any dead bodies out there now?" asked John hesitantly.

"Yes, I think you walked past three."

"Four," said Frank quickly, "the other one was ready at the mortuary, so I thought it best to bring it and save a trip."

"Why didn't you show me any then?" asked the new face.

"All in good time." I said, "The best way to start is when you're expecting to and not just to walk in here and see a body just for the sake of it. Anyway, we have got to see how you drive first."

We finished up our tea and I took John out to the van to see how he handled a vehicle. It is quite easy to evaluate a person's driving on any vehicle without risking possible disaster with one of the limousines.

He made a passable effort and I offered him to start whenever he could and asked whether he had a dark suit for the first few days. This is another problem with staff, they have to be dressed well to act as funeral drivers, jeans and sneakers is frowned upon by the relatives for some reason. Luckily, he fitted an old, though tatty black suit of mine, this would do for starters and for his first week's trial as he might not be able to cope with the job or me with him.

We did two days trial later that week, which went well enough to start full-time on the following Monday. He even had his hair cut. Frank, John and I worked together for about eighteen months and we had our differences but succeeded in getting the work done well enough and on time.

Eventually and I do not know whether it was the fact that his girlfriend didn't like the idea of his handling the dead and her or the given reason as the better job. Both reasons existed but I never knew which came first. He did have the courtesy to tell me that he was looking for a new job and give me plenty of notice, for this, I have always respected him.

The most memorable trick I ever played on him started with his failure to be able to understand and remember how the coffin linings were put in, he had some sort of a jinx that would always end up with something being either left out or put in wrongly. We had been busy and Frank had a few hours off because one of his children was ill. I asked John to finish the coffin linings before he went home. He finished it and left. The job was just about perfect.

That evening, whilst having a late night drink in the pub next door, a man came in selling large stuffed toy animals. I bought one as a birthday present for a small child. It was a dog with a huge nose. First thing in the morning, I took 'Phideaux' out to the workshops and stuffed him tightly into the coffin that John had prepared the night before. When Frank showed that morning, I told him of my wicked little plan. John arrived.

"John, first thing, go and finish off that coffin lining, would you?" Logic should have told him that if he had not finished it the night before, I would have done so.

"It's done. I did it before I went last night," he replied, hurt. "Well, you go out there, have a look at it and tell me that it's done."

I had a tone of annoyance in my voice. We had had this sort of conversation before and he had always come off worst. This time, the job he had completed was fine and I had the impression that he had made certain that everything was just so before he had left the previous evening.

"Well, what's wrong with it then, inside or outside?" Very hurt indeed.

"You go out there and you tell me," I replied arrogantly.

We both marched out together, Frank appeared at the other end of the workshop at just the right time. "You've let me down again, sunshine," he said to John.

"What's the matter with it," said John, walking round the coffin standing on its trestles counting handles, wreath holders, plate, ornaments etc., as he opened the lid, virtually in tears, dear old Phideaux sprung back to shape to the open-mouthed amazement of our John, whose feet had instantly decided to leave whether his body was ready or not, the coffin lid had also seen what was going on and leapt safely from John's hands into Frank's without giving notice.

Two of us collapsed into tearful mirth at the expense of our colleague who started to storm off in anger, I caught his arm and we walked off to tea together. John was not the same all that day and it was obvious that we had not only annoyed him, but also frightened him more than I would have expected. As time went by, he began to deny the fact that he had been so shocked but I still remember his face in that single instant. Anyway, Frank and I enjoyed ourselves immensely.

Eddie was the next lamb for slaughter and was quite a different person, a few years older than I and having been a bookie's settler for many years was a genius at mental arithmetic, although more cumbersome and expensive than a pocket calculator, he beat the 'Casio' hands down when it came to making tea.

The interview was a different thing altogether, with the exception of the ring at the doorbell. I opened the door. "Mr Moss? Eddie Rogan, come about the job. Yes, come in, take a seat in the office."

He sat down fairly relaxed but not slouching. We chatted for some time about the requirements of the job and the training he would be given. He had not driven for some time and had never driven anything larger than a saloon car, it was obvious that I was dealing with an intelligent man so I felt that this would come with time. We then came to discussing the last and not insignificant part about the handling of the dead. His attitude was the approach of a logical mind, although somewhat misguided.

"Well, you are obviously quite used to it and you seem to be quite normal so I have nothing to worry about!"

I thought about the people I knew in the funeral trade for a second and could not bring to mind any person who would fit under that heading of 'normal', however, I did need a driver and he looked as if any initial shock could be overcome by administration of alcohol. The other thing that swayed me to offer him a job was the fact that he was the only person to have answered the advertisement in weeks.

I offered him the job. He then met Frank, who was his normal cheery and friendly self as we talked over the inevitable cup of tea. We decided that there was no time like the present and we had a collection to do from the local mortuary and it seemed more likely that Frank, not being the boss, would be the better person to carry out the initial appraisal of the new man's driving abilities.

At the time, our van was being resprayed and therefore the hearse was being used as removal vehicle, this beast, a princess with a column gear change for a manual gearbox was not the easiest car to drive, it's one score years and five had naturally taken toll of the gear linkage with so many joints, knuckles and rods that the stick itself had about as much feel as a dessert spoon in a bowl of lumpy porridge, this, added to the fact that Eddie had not driven for some time, the vehicle was large, valuable and someone else's struck untold fear into the poor guy's every corpuscle.

I left Frank to deal with the whole driving affair after having a quick word with him. "Take him around the area a bit before going to the mortuary to get him used to the car and you drive back in case he is shaken up by the place."

"No problem, we don't have much else to do today, we'll go and fill it up with petrol first so he can get to know his way around," said Frank thoughtfully, "And by the way, how come I never got a driving test, was it because I had been in the trade before and knew how to drive the cars?"

"Something like that and I didn't want to make the same mistake again!"

"Thanks a bunch!" he said as he went.

Some considerable time later, I heard them return and went to find out how Eddie had got on with the car.

"How was the mortuary?" I asked Ed.

"Interesting, interesting," he said with a little uncertainty in his voice. "I expect it will take a little time to get used to," he said with a resignation that meant he was not going to be frightened off easily.

I glanced over at Frank as I asked Ed how he felt about the driving, Frank shook his head in despair and it was clear that the car had been unfriendly, obstinate or both. "It's going to take a little time to get used to those gears," said Ed with a little less certainty than before.

Frank's face indicated that "a little time" was likely to be this lifetime and most of the next, we went for tea and a chat.

We talked for a while and tried to find out exactly what he was having problems with and it seemed to be, the gear change, the size of the car, the fact that it was not his car, not forgetting that he was shaking like a leaf. I decided that tomorrow would be another day and said that he could start at nine and we would try again.

From the look on Ed's face, it was obvious that he had expected the offer of a job to have been rescinded. A smile swept over him.

"You mean to say that I've gone out in your car and made a complete fool of myself and you are still offering me a job?" he said in disbelief.

"Yes, we've got a couple of days before our next funeral is out and I am sure we can train you up by then," I replied, not forgetting the sheer number of other applicants for the job.

He was very grateful as he left and assured me that he would not let me down.

The next day, the hearse was being similarly obstinate to our Ed and the ease of demonstration from Frank was serving to exasperate the new man even more, I struck upon a new idea. Frank was the hearse driver and this was his car, it was also the older car and more worn out than the limousine that Eddie would be driving most of the time as his job.

"Get the 'Lim' out and let him have a go on that," I said to Frank. With the end of the day approaching, we swapped the cars about and off they went with instructions not to come back until he could drive. It was getting towards evening when they returned. I looked at Ed. "Can you drive it tomorrow?" I asked.

"Yes, I think so," he said confidently.

Over the next few years, Eddie turned out to be an excellent driver, a valued employee and, more than that, a good mate. During the early days, at the weekends, he would go back to his old stamping grounds in North London and on two of these occasions returned for work on the Monday morning, slightly battle scarred.

The first of these times he walked in with a huge bruise below one eye turning to varying shades from yellow to black, Frank and I looked at each other in horror since we had to go out on a funeral within the next hour and thought that this was not the image we wanted to give the public. We had, apparently, been standing in the wrong place in a pub in Enfield when a fist that had been travelling at high speed came to an abrupt halt. Frank called his wife Christine and said that we needed a makeup artist, Eddie was duly whisked away to have his face painted. He returned looking much better, although a little more like a repertory actor than a funeral assistant.

The very next Monday, he arrived for work with face scratched from forehead to chin with multiple contusions and the backs of both his hands similarly damaged, he was also limping.

"What on earth happened to you?" Frank and I looked on, open-mouthed.

"Well, it's like this," he started. "When I left here on Friday night, I was waiting for the bus when it started to rain, I didn't have a coat as I had left it here and there was this pub offering dry warm shelter right next to me. Not being one to be able to resist temptation for long, I weakened. If you remember, it did rain for almost the whole evening and, not wanting to get a chill, I waited." He was certainly cheerful enough.

"Whatever has that to do with the state of you," I enquired, thinking that this was going to be a long story.

"Well, as you know, I take my ex-wife some money on Fridays and it was now getting late, they kicked us out of the pub and I caught the last bus which only went to Ponders End so I had to walk the last three miles. I got some fish 'n' chips and then started walking. Well, it was getting cold so I had my hands in my pockets, walking along 'appy as a sandboy whistling to myself. Being suitable refreshed, I couldn't have been watching where I was putting my feet and stubbed my toe on the edge of a paving stone. I was not quick enough to get the other foot forward and down I went, with my hands stuck firmly in my pockets. There was nothing I could do to save myself."

We both laughed at our colleague's misfortune and shipped him off to Christine to have his face repaired.

Both Eddie and Frank were conscientious and willing workers and together, undoubtedly the best crew I ever had. Eddie lived some twelve miles away and Frank lived about a hundred yards away. A common early morning conversation went something like this.

"Frank, every morning, I catch two buses and walk for half an hour and get here by about twenty to nine and you're always late for work?"

"Well, Ed, if you wake up late, you can skip breakfast, dress quickly, dash out and still catch the bus. If I wake up late, I'm already late for work!"

"But Frank, I don't eat breakfast, anyway. I get up at six thirty, make the tea, wash, dress and catch the same bus every day, rain or shine and I'm always here at the same time."

"Ed, you don't understand, my normal time for getting up is eight thirty and it takes me twenty minutes to get ready and I plan to get here by about five to nine."

"So how come when I knock on your door every morning at ten past nine, you're still in bed." The sarcasm in the voice is increasing.

"There you are, if I am half an hour late in getting up, I'm already late for work, if you are half an hour late, then it's still only seven and you have two hours to get to work." Frank would say, sounding very reasonable.

"Frank, if I get up at seven then my daughter is in the bathroom before me and I can't get in there till half past and the bus gets caught in the traffic and I would not arrive at work until half-past nine and I am never late. You are late nearly every day. How about getting up in the morning?" The tone would become fierce but the sarcasm and humour would remain genuine.

This would happen at least once a month and various bets would be placed, usually in the form of tobacco as to who would be in at work first for the next full week, I cannot remember if Frank ever won but I don't think that Eddie ever collected either.

On one occasion, when a bus strike was planned for the following day, Eddie promised faithfully that he would be on time as we had a funeral going out in the morning. It was a warm and sunny morning in May when Eddie arrived at his normal time of about twenty to nine and had already been to Frank's door to make sure he was up, he wasn't. When Frank turned up just before nine, the banter started with more vigour than usual.

"Frank," said Ed gravely, "I had to walk here this morning and left home at a quarter to six and when I got here, you were still in bed!"

"Well, I was up at six as well and took my boy to school as there were no buses and I wasn't in bed when you called. I was in the bathroom. You see, I can get up when I have to," said Frank triumphantly.

"But you can't get up just for work!" I put my penny's worth in.

"Oh, but I'm always here when there is work to be done," replied Frank in a very hurt manner.

"Only with a little help from your friends," said Ed.

"Ed?" I asked, "Why didn't you take the train from Enfield to Clapton, it was only the buses that were on strike." Eddie's mouth dropped open.

"Were the trains running?" asked Ed in amazement.

"Yes." Frank butted in, "Didn't you know?" he asked with glee.

"Do you mean to say that I have walked for three hours to get here on time when I could have taken the train directly." The tables had been turned and Frank wasn't going to let this one go easily.

"Oh Ed they said on the radio that there were so many people taking the day off that the trains were running on time and were not overcrowded." Ed took the train home that night.

Frank, Eddie and I worked together for about two years until Frank was 'poached' by another undertaker from out of town. We had had dealings with this man since he had work in our area and we provided him with cars for a funeral, during the months following that first job, we assisted the same person on several occasions.

Unfortunately, this resulted in Frank going to work for the other undertaker at the time when I was just beginning to appreciate the crew that I had and also, we were starting to increase our work that would enable me to reward them for their hard work and loyalty over the years. Even worse for Frank, the grass on the other side turned out not to be as green as promised and soon withered and died, leaving him stranded far from his roots. Later, he took up embalming so our paths crossed again.

Following Frank's departure, the inevitable advertisement was placed with the job centre, resulting in the usual non-existent line of smart young potentials pleading to become a funeral assistant.

Eventually, along came Bill, a large man from Scotland of about the same age as Eddie and myself. Bill worked for about six months and left quite suddenly. Ed and I then worked for many months using casual staff, mainly in the form of uncle Bob, my old friend Graham. Graham had been in the funeral trade for much longer than I had and, being about the same age, we had made firm friends some years before and shared the same sense of humour, rotten.

Another friend of mine, David, was, at this time, thinking of buying his own limousine and doing limousine hire work, weddings and funerals. I had said that he could keep a car in my garage and that he could have my second car work if that was what he wanted to do.

It was late one Sunday evening in the winter when the telephone rang, it was the coroner's officer and could I do a removal for him to the public mortuary, everything was ready, the doctor had been and the family, who wanted us to make the arrangements were at the home waiting for us. As was the normal course of events, I called the family to let them know that I would be there when I had found a member of my staff to assist me. This on a Sunday could be easier said than done, however it would always be possible to call another undertaker and borrow a man for the job. This was one of the greatest things about the funeral trade at that time, people would help without question, whoever they worked for.

This evening, I could find none of my staff, Eddie was out, Graham was incognito, Bob was visiting friends in Essex and I was about to call the opposition when I remembered David, who lived two doors away. I knocked on his door.

"How do you fancy earning twenty quid?" That should help his mind in the right direction, I thought. The corners of his mouth made considerable progress in the direction of his ears. So far so good.

"How do I do that?" he asked in a guarded way. I knew the next bit would be a mite more tricky.

"Oh, just come for a little ride with me in the van," I said innocently.

"Let me get this straight, you are going to pay me twenty quid just to sit next to you whilst you drive around in your van." I was beginning to think that he was suspecting something.

"You could drive if you like," I said, trying to be nonchalant.

"Julian," he said, "You're hiding something from me, aren't you! I think you are forgetting that I know what you do for a living."

"Ok, I admit it, after we have been driving about for long enough, I will let you buy me a pint!" It was worth a try.

"I still think there is something you're not telling me." This guy was really suspicious, I tried pathos.

"Trust me!" I pleaded. "No." emphatically, "I know you too well."

"Well, OK, there is a dead body involved."

"How big?"

"Well, that's nice, your first body and you want to know what the rate is going to be by the kilo. That's mercenary and I thought you were my friend."

"OK, but what's it going to look like?"

"It can't 'LOOK' at all, David, that's why we've got the job," I intimated, "Didn't you see the 'Parrot sketch'?"

"I didn't mean that, I meant, what is the body going to look like to me!" he said, assuming now that I was more than a little insane.

"Oh," I said with surprise, "Just like yours, older; more female, in fact, a lot more female; more horizontal, probably; less active, just and it will most likely smell worse." I then remembered stumbling across a dirty sock one day in his flat, "On second thoughts, forget the last bit."

Terms agreed, which entailed vast quantities of alcohol, we then went through the wardrobe at the shop to find our David something dark and suit like to wear for the great occasion. I made a point of buying my staff their suits and overcoats so that they matched in style and texture, it had become normal practice to leave these at work and change when required.

"This is ridiculous," said David.

"Those suits are perfectly normal, it's you that is the ridiculous shape."

We settled for Bill's old suit, which, although reached both wrists and ankles, would have gone around him more than once. We made some quick alterations with string so that the trousers would at least leave him one arm free to work with. Now our David is not the sort of person who could be described as 'dapper' but the result was 'hanging' to say the least.

"Never mind," I said. "It would look fine at night at a Guide Dog's Convention."

"You're so flattering, Julian. No wonder your friends ignore you." And off we went.

At the apartment, third floor, no lift and a tightly, turning stairway, I went upstairs alone first to meet the family and put them at their ease before sneaking the "tailor's delight" in and out as fast as possible. With all the attributes listed above, it was quite a shock to find the reason for our sortie at less than twenty stone, she was much nearer to 'petite'.

"Shell only for this one." I said, as I reached David, patiently waiting at the van.

"What's it like?" he couldn't wait to know.

"Well, it's about twenty stone, been dead about three months, claret all over the floor and smells like a herd of haddock that's been hiding for six months in a fridge full of rotten onions."

"You're kidding," he said as his face shone out on bright green against the reflected glow of the sodium streetlights, an unusual contrast with white shirt and baggy suit. We went up.

"Just one more," I said as we arrived at every floor until there were no more. I took young David into the flat to put him out of his misery. He had obviously noticed the smirk on my face during the ascent and, although relieved, was not surprised to find the object of our journey clean and lightweight. We had just lifted her into the shell when the string holding his trousers up gave way.

"Oh, shit!" said David, grabbing at his falling trousers.

"Where?" I asked, being more used to the job I couldn't resist the obvious reply whilst trying to restrain myself from collapsing into a fit of the giggles. We looked at each other not daring to breathe in case we laughed and then not daring to look at each other for the same reason, relatives were in the next room and we could not make any noise let alone release the laughter building in both our lungs.

As silently as the escaping titters of mirth would allow, we took our charge out and down the stairs, stopping at each flight to take the nearest thing to a deep breath we dared before continuing. I didn't dare look at David clutching at the waistband of his outsize and uncooperative strides whilst trying to negotiate the stairway and hold on to the shell. When we did arrive at the van, it was with the greatest relief that we slid the shell into the back before getting away as fast as possible to allow the release of our giggles.

Normally, I would have gone back into the house and told the family that we had finished and bid them goodbye but on this one occasion, I didn't dare because I didn't think I could do it straight faced. This, as far as I can remember, was the only time that I was unable to go back into the house.

We arrived at the police station where we would have to collect the keys for the mortuary and I wonder what they thought when I walked in with tears streaming down my face and asked for them. When he asked what was so funny, the vision of David that few moments before returned, bringing on further tears and laughter. "Strange people these undertakers," was written all over the policeman's face.

With the job done and van parked, we made haste to the public house, stopping for enough time only to change back to more normal attire.

It was not long before David had bought a limousine, moved it into my garage and started to share my second office. I gave him what work I could and he drove for me when I needed a driver, this worked well for some time. He made quite a number of connections in the car hire trade, which gave him some interesting jobs.

We covered these with the care we had and on occasions, this would result in some lucky person booking a Daimler for the evening and having a Rolls Royce turn up. We never had any complaints about this, however, I did suspect one would normally send the Rolls. We took great pleasure in hiring in a friend's Daimler to do the job and it certainly caused the unscrupulous agent the intended headache.

With David's car hire work building up well and my gaining a contract with another local funeral director to supply his cars, it was coming to the time when I would need another driver myself. I was then lucky enough to receive a telephone call from a young man called Steve, who was working for another local firm but wanted to move. I agreed to interview him.

Steve arrived at my office on the Saturday morning, he was a smart dresser and already had his own black suit, his hair in a short neat Afro style and a row of condemned tombstones where his teeth had once been. We talked for a while and it was clear to me that he had the normal sarcasm associated with the workers of the trade.

We went for a drive, which was a pleasure and I assumed that he was being a little overcautious for the sake of the 'test'. After discussing the matter with David, since a new permanent employee would take some of his livelihood, I offered Steve to start when convenient to him and a date was agreed.

In the sleepy funeral trade of the east of London, news permeates at a leisurely pace. Steve had started at nine on the Monday and had gone out on removals with Eddie shortly after. Before 10 o'clock the telephone rang, it was the manager of yet another local undertaker, a good friend who originated from Scotland.

"Morning, Julian, I see you have been stealing employees!" said the Scotsman.

"Hi Dave, what makes you say that?" I said calmly.

"Well, I've just seen your van out on removals with Eddie sitting in the passenger seat and a 'cuddly toy' driving." From that day, the name stuck, although abbreviated to 'CT'.

Eddie, Steve and David got on as well as could be expected with any three men working in close proximity. Steve was a natural 'fall guy' and with his ability to see humour in just about any situation, kept us all entertained. Being the 'new boy' on the firm, he would assume himself to be the lowest form of life in existence and any request he might have would usually be heralded by a preamble such as:

"Sir, fully aware, as I am, of being the lowest form of existence in the universe and with aspirations of reaching the status of a slug and if I have taken up too much of your time already, please instruct me to flail myself alive being sure to take myself to the crematorium, at my own expense of course, before dying."

"You want something, don't you?" I would always have to butt in.

"Yes." Would be the blunt reply with an empty silence following.

"Would there be any chance of relating this request in simple English?" The tirade would continue.

"My sincerest apologies, sir, oh most elevated one, for wasting your valuable time with such irrelevancies."

"Steve—!"

"Yes, sir."

"Stick something large and sound absorbing in it!"

"Yes, sir."

"Using just ONE word, can you tell me what you want?" This would often be the only way to get the better of him at these times.

"Yes—" Well, I supposed I had asked for it. "What is it you need?"

"Milk." I gave him some money to get the milk for the afternoon tea.

This sort of complication would happen at one end of his humour scale, at the other end, I remember doing a removal with him when his comment was a short mixed cliché that reflected his own personal view of the futility of existence itself.

We were standing in an apartment where all the furniture was ancient, torn and crumbling, dirty rags that had once been curtains hung from excuses for curtain rails, odd part-empty food cartons scattered on tables and floors, an array of milk bottles were growing the same fungi all at different stages and a grimy handleless mug on the floor by the bed with the half worn out logo that had once proudly stated, 'I LOVE MY DAD'.

Add to this the discoloured rotting unrecognisable remains of a human being, half on and half off a bed surrounded by a pool of decaying fluid and a stench that seemed to have the ability to strangle you from the inside.

Just inside the doorway stood Steve, hands in trouser pockets, the hem of his jacket flopping over each forearm, he looked at me with a sarcastic smile and said cheerily, "Well, I suppose we ought to blame both the parents and the government for this one!"

CT's rotund face and body soon earned him a different nickname from Eddie, who started calling Steve, 'Our little fat friend' or 'Porky'. The latter stuck fast and his hated name spread about the trade to his dismay. There was nothing he could do to shake it.

He had been working for me for some time when his teeth, what was left of them, started bothering him, it was obvious to me that he was not only self-conscious about his teeth but also frightened of dentists. It so happened that a friend of mine was the local dentist and a very good one too. I offered to pay for Porky's new smile and take a certain amount from his pay per week.

"Does he do a 'while you wait service' or will I have to leave my mouth for a week?" was about as much sense as I could expect.

After many discussions and a great deal of goading, he braved his fear and went. The result was thereafter known as 'Moss's Molars'.

"Of course, you realise what's going to happen," said Eddie one day. "When he gets the new set, he's never going to stop smiling. He'll probably start wearing loud suits, playing the piano and talking funnier than he does now."

The company chompers were duly fitted and Porks did indeed go about smiling at all and sundry. "Are we going to have company sunglasses issued for the glare?" asked Ed one day.

Over the years, other staff came and left but none were as fun or as memorable as Frank, Eddie, Steve, Graham and David. All the above could be relied upon on those days when it was pouring with rain or sleet and we had a burial that was going to take most of the afternoon and to respond correctly to the little voice that said, "It's not a very nice day for it?"

The rousing chorus in reply would always be:

DON'T BE BLOODY RIDICULOUS, EVERY DAY IS A NICE DAY FOR A FUNERAL!

--

Chapter Eight
The Delaney Mob

There was always one job in one's life that stands out as being quite different to all the others and this often follows with one specific funeral with an undertaker. For some, it will be the time that they went to the wrong cemetery. Sometimes, it will be the funeral of the country's heaviest man, the dropping of a coffin, an accident, breakdown or some other horrendous event.

For me, thankfully, it was none of the above. The funeral I will always remember above all others, nearly had a breakdown but didn't quite, the relatives were very pleased with everything we did but had one tragic loss for me, I lost my favourite hammer. It is not as bad as it sounds, please read on.

It all started in a February one year when I received a call from the daughter of a woman who had died at home in Clapton. From the outset, it had all the hallmarks of being a nuisance job. Firstly, they did not want Mum to be removed from the house or to go to our chapel. Secondly, they wanted a solid oak coffin that we did not keep in stock and would have to order and what with a church service and the re-open of a grave in St Patrick's looked to be and drawn out affair.

I went to the house, it was dull, dark and it desperately needed painting. There was oilcloth on the floor of indeterminate age, everything was old. The normal gloom clouded over me and I did not know what to expect from the people. This is the sort of place horror movies start from, it looked for all the world that dear old mum had been left alone to fend for herself for years but there were two things wrong with that theory, the place was clean and didn't smell.

I met Teresa, the eldest and sister Christine, who showed me into the front room where Mum was on the bed, all beautifully clean and laid out, it was obvious that someone had had some medical training. I took initial details and left to make these arrangements firm with the cemetery and the church and also to arrange for an embalmer to go to the house and perform his art.

I knew that none of them liked working in people's houses, not only because of the lack of facilities but also accidents do happen and when things go wrong, they can leave a dramatic-looking mess resulting from the tiniest slip. If a vein breaks, it will leave a lot of dark red blood about which will always be attracted to the whitest sheet and cover the largest area.

Within the workshop, this is a simple matter to clear up and the repair is made with a little shot of specialist powder but in the home, having to ask to use the bathroom or kitchen to wash off copious quantities of red stuff can have varied effects on already distraught relatives. The embalmer went and left without incident, to my great relief.

The coffin arrived and we took it to the house complete with identification plate 'CHRISTINA DELANEY', date of death and age. Mum was placed in the coffin and the gown put on, the coffin placed on trestles, best pall cover over the top.

I now met the rest of the family. So far, I had met Teresa and Christine and I was now introduced to the two sons Christopher and Tommy. It seemed to me that there were a large number of Chris's in the family and I was told that confusion was allayed by the fact that Christopher was nicknamed 'Dibbey', where this name came from, I did not dare ask. The greeting and pleasantries over, we left.

I was beginning to warm to this family, firstly there were four of them as with my own, secondly they all talked at the same time whilst understanding the conversations of each other and lastly, they were polite and friendly even though somewhat confusing to outsiders.

The funeral was arranged for some days later when we would be collecting the coffin from the house and taking it to the church the day before the funeral. Disasters apart, I did not expect to see the family again until that time.

I received a telephone call the very next day, it was Teresa. "You've spelt mum's name wrong!"

"No, I didn't. I spelt it as on the arrangements form and the green certificate from the registrar."

"Well, it's wrong, mum's name was Christine, can we have it changed please!" she asked curtly.

"I thought your sister's name was Christine and mum was Christina," I interjected politely.

"Well, no, it isn't, we should know our own names!" she pointed out unarguably. I had to agree that although the official forms did say Christina.

"I'm sorry but I am bound by the spelling of the names on the registrar's forms and that is what we will have to use," I said a little aggressively and thinking to myself that this woman was going to be a nuisance. "If you want it changed, you will have to start with the town hall." As I said it I felt a little mean.

"Oh, I'm sorry Mr Moss but couldn't you just change the name on the coffin, just for us?" asked Teresa in just the right tone at just the right time, how could refuse. I engraved another plate and took it round to the house that evening and felt a much better person for having done so.

The next day, the telephone rang again. Teresa again, I recognised her voice immediately knew she was annoyed. What now, I thought, have they decided to change their mother's name yet again. I was beginning to wonder how many derivatives of Chris there were.

"The age is wrong," she said firmly.

"No, it isn't. I've got your mother's age down here as 84 years," I replied glibly.

"Yes and it says 82 on the coffin." She had me again so I took another nameplate to the house that evening This time it did not make me feel any better at all.

The day of taking it into church arrived and I was relieved to be able to seal the coffin for the last time. When a body is lying in our chapel, we could always keep a good eye on it to make sure that there are no leaks or unpleasantness before relatives view, however this cannot be done at home and there was always that doubt at the back of my mind that something would go wrong and gossip would spread about the neighbourhood resulting in bad feelings toward the business, especially my own.

We took the coffin out of the house and loaded it and the flowers into the hearse, somebody had locked the house with the trestles inside. I remember thinking that it was a good thing we noticed this at the time and not at the church. A silly thought went through my mind of the bearers standing in the church still holding the coffin during the service because we had nothing else to put it on.

The remainder of that evening was quite normal, it was usual to arrive at that church to find it locked and have to go and wake the priest up to open the church and begin the service. This entailed a lengthy walk and a wait for the mourners.

The next morning, we arrived at the house to collect the family. This was normal practice, it being a convenient meeting place for people to bring flowers and make their way to the church in a normal procession. I was not surprised to find that they had all gone to church early. We made our way to the church and met the family there, standing outside a locked church, again no surprise.

The rest of the funeral went smoothly, we arrived at the cemetery on time and took the family home afterwards. I was plied with much gratitude and alcohol. The job did have its compensations.

The funeral bill was paid promptly and as far as I was concerned, the job was done. I had met some pleasant people and we might get the job to renovate the stone in the near future.

It was June and therefore some surprise that my receptionist told me that Teresa and Tommy had been in asking for me. They had not come in about the memorial but a 'delicate matter'. They had been insistent on seeing me and I wondered what awful surprise awaited me. The worst thing that could have happened, though unlikely, was that we had buried the coffin in the wrong grave. It was so long after the funeral that it would not be the usual things like the fact that the flowers were not put on the grave.

Did they leave an umbrella in the car or a glove or lose a piece of jewellery and would it be in the car? These things were common enough and we usually spotted lost items first and returned them immediately. I had to wait.

When we met, their request took me back more than a little. They wanted to have both Mum and Dad exhumed and taken home to Eire from where they had both come. I had been aware that they had stretched themselves financially to pay for the funeral and had insisted on a solid oak coffin rather than the cheaper veneered chipboard variety. Now they wanted to spend a vast sum of money on something that was, in essence, unnecessary. Their logic behind this was quite beautiful.

When their father had died in 1957, Mother had wanted to send him back home but had not been able to afford it with the children to look after. Now, the children had decided that they would sell the house, in which they had all lived through some period of their life and use some of the proceeds to grant their parents' last wishes.

Although I had attended an exhumation in the past, I had never made arrangements for such a thing and with the added problem of international transportation. I felt duty bound to inform them that the cost would be high. They said that they had realised that it would be expensive and we agreed that I would prepare a rough estimate for them before making their final decision and that the estimate would not be binding.

In my spare time over the next few weeks, I put together a very rough estimate for the cost of the double exhumation from St Patrick's, providing new sealed coffins and the transportation by closed vehicle to Waterford, the service in the Basilica there and the burial in a new private grave in a little cemetery just outside their home village.

The numbers on the estimate frightened me but did not seem to worry them one little bit. What did worry them was how they were expected to get to Waterford themselves, since they did not have a car or driving licence between them. They asked me to arrange their transport as well and add it to the estimate.

When I had done this, the figure looked even more daunting. Teresa and Dibbey came in and I told them the rough estimate. They both agreed that it sounded reasonable but were not very happy with their own transport arrangements as they might get lost or the changes of transport required would give them added worry that they did not want.

Finally, I suggested that we could take the hearse, limousine and them as a cortege, all the way from Hackney to Waterford. They virtually agreed on the spot but I insisted on presenting them with an estimate. Teresa, I think, now noticed that I was a little concerned about the eventual payment of the account and as they were not in a position to leave me with a substantial deposit. She offered to get the solicitor to write and confirm that the house was for sale and that he was aware of their intentions. It was, after all, now becoming a very substantial commitment.

It was finally agreed that we would all travel together with the hearse, limousine and the two coffins and we tentatively arranged a date for some time in late September for the journey.

The next step was to apply to the Home Office for permission to exhume the two bodies. The forms were duly filled out with a myriad of signatures. My own as the applicant to take the responsibility for public health regulations and finances; that of the cemetery superintendent to allow the exhumation in the event of the Home Office granting permission and that of the owner of the grave expressing the wish that the whole thing take place. The form clearly stated that permission could take anything from six to ten weeks and it was not possible to enter into any telephone discussions on the matter—in the normal, helpful governmental manner.

A trip was made to St. Catherine's house to obtain any number of copies of the death certificates for both parties; to the coroner's office in the area of the burial for the required permission to remove the bodies outside the United Kingdom. The file was growing in size daily.

The regulations for exhumation include the provision of a new coffin and whilst I had the dimensions of the coffin we had used for Mum, that of dad's presented a little more of a problem.

"Morning, John, flip your mind back to 1957, St Anthony's Plot grave number 138, what was the size of the old fella's coffin," I asked the cemetery superintendent.

"Was that the morning or afternoon job, Julian? I can't quite remember." Sarcasm abounds.

A search of the cemetery records drew a blank on the coffin size for that interment. It was worth a try.

I ordered two coffins from our supplier, one with inside dimensions of the same as the outside dimensions of the coffin we had buried earlier that year and a very large one, just in case. When they arrived with our next delivery, the small one took on boat-like proportions whilst the larger one was positively titanic.

The job of lining these in metal for international transport began, bit by bit. This was rather a pleasant change for me, having three months' notice of a funeral is unheard of. Well, it wouldn't seem right would it, even the initial phone call would be positively 'Pythonesque'.

"Hello, is that the undertaker?"

"Yes, sir and how may we help you?"

"Well, it's about my uncle!"

"I see, sir, your uncle has passed away. And where has the death occurred?"

"Er, well, he hasn't, not yet but he will, Er."

"Yes, sir, we all have to, it's one of the problems of being born. It's rather like having a glass of beer, it has to come to an end at some time."

"Er, yes, well, he will die soon and we just wondered whether you could come round, measure him up, sort of quietly so he doesn't know."

This brings to mind all sorts of mental pictures of people in suits creeping round hospitals and homes with tape measures trying to look casual.

The coffins were lined with the accompanying lacerations to my arms, now perceived as normal when working with metal. There was no need to provide anything to hold the inside linings as I thought that nobody would want to view either body, well I certainly didn't.

The weeks went by until early August, I had found out the times of the ferries from Fishguard to Rosslare but not made any bookings in case the Home Office had decided to decline our request or the six to ten weeks extended to the sum of those numbers. Contact had been made with an undertaker in Waterford who was very willing to help, although changed the subject whenever it came to discussing the cost of his services.

The family came into the office again, I informed them of progress so far and intimated that all was on schedule so long as the governmental paperwork was forthcoming. They then came in with another request.

"What about the memorial?" asked Teresa.

I had not even thought about it, as I had assumed that they would make their own arrangements in the time to come after the funeral. "We have a perfectly good memorial already with father's name on it in St Patrick's cemetery."

Now this memorial was six foot six by three feet with a headstone some three feet in height and had once been a very beautiful and expensive memorial stone. It was now thirty years old and although not marked with any stains was very pitted and eroded, however, they did have a point. I said I would inspect the stone and prepare an estimate for its renovation but that there was no chance that we could take the whole thing without taking another vehicle just for the stone.

Also, that it was not a good idea to put a new full head to foot memorial on a grave immediately after the burial as the ground would settle and possible tip the memorial to unsafe angles.

The criterion here was whether it would be cheaper to renovate and transport the existing memorial or buy a new one in Ireland at a later date. After making some enquiries for renovation versus new, it came out quite favourably on the side of renovation.

I was able to provide the family with the existing stone renovated, newly lettered with two new flower vases and a free standing bible with a new verse for the same cost as the headstone in Ireland. A very expensive country is Ireland. The renovation order went in and was added to the estimate. The current estimate in comparison to the very first I had prepared was all but stupefying. The family accepted the latest figure without the bat of an eyelid.

The paperwork eventually arrived from the Home Office, this meant that it was definitely going to happen so we booked some dates, cemeteries, one at each end of the journey, public health officer, the undertaker at the end and the church, ferry crossings and a hotel for both us and the family not forgetting the man who was working on the memorial, 'Ray the Stone'. The time approached.

Regulations covering exhumations include such things as: "The exhumation will be carried out as early in the morning as practical," this seemed to me to be about ten thirty so that the pubs would be open just as you finished the job as it sounded a perfect time to be in great need of a drink.

However, what they actually mean is the time of early morning fog when one has decided to take a shortcut home through the woods from a very late night party when a twig some distance off to you left will loudly say 'CRACK' soliciting an immediate 'CAW' from the crow on your right and you turn to look nervously behind you to stop the person who isn't there from putting their hand on your shoulder.

"The act will be suitably screened from public view" and "It is the responsibility of the applicant to request the attendance of the local public health officer," "The authority of the bishop of the diocese will be sought" and "The remains shall be sanitised and a certificate confirming this will be issued for inspection."

The idea of an embalmer getting to grips with a body that had been in the ground for that length of time somehow horrified me and I was very glad when it was suggested that we use a strong powdered form of the embalming fluid. This stuff is lethal to everything and must be treated with the greatest respect.

Even the tiniest spot on your clothing can release the strongest, though fresh, odour that lingers until the garment is cleaned. I often used to wonder what my dry cleaner thought of my job as I would arrive with my clothing smelling of various things, some pleasant, some very unpleasant but always powerful. I was thankful over the years to lose my sense of smell almost completely.

The plan was to firstly bring Mum up one day and dad on the following, this was done to allow plenty of time in case we ran into difficulties. The morning arrived and surprisingly enough it wasn't foggy at all but it was pouring with rain, we raised the coffin quite easily and slotted it into the new coffin and sanitised the whole thing with the powder, much to the interest of the public health officer who had not seen the powder before. He agreed with us that it would not be a good idea to smell it as a way of inspection. In view of the unpleasant weather, I was very glad that he trusted me to finish sealing the coffin for transportation at my own workshop. One up, one to go.

The next day was comparatively boring, the sun was shining and birds twittering, the coffin came up without any trouble at all, it was in surprisingly good condition, we slipped it into the new box and sealed that down, in fact there was nothing to grumble at, at all.

It was the Thursday morning before we were due to leave on the Monday and all we were waiting for was the memorial. When I did find 'Ray the Stone', the job was not done. "You'll have to get your skates on, I want to load this lot onto the cars on Saturday at the latest," I told him.

"I thought you were leaving on Monday, I was going to bring them over to you then," he said, oblivious of the other loading and planning that were required for the trip.

"Yes, I am and I shall be rolling down the Balls Pond Road before 6 a.m. and I have no interest to be loading the whole lot up late on Sunday night."

Stonework is rather like having your shoes repaired, you find a three-year-old ticket in your wardrobe, take it to the menders out of curiosity to see which shoes they actually were, assuming that they have long been discarded when the cobbler takes a glance at the ticket and says, "They'll be ready Wednesday."

We settled for Saturday about lunchtime and, rather than have any problems with transportation, I insisted that I would collect it from him. I arrived and waited. Luckily, there was a handy pub for lunch, otherwise I would have been very annoyed when we eventually loaded at three fifteen.

Into the lower deck of the hearse went a toolbox, just in case, the stone bible, some cement, stone erecting tools and one coffin with the other coffin in full view on the top deck. The headstone and base went into the boot of the limousine, leaving room for clothing bags of the eight people who were going to take the journey both ways.

A telephone call on the Sunday to let me know that one of my drivers, Eddie, was in hospital with chest pains drove me to a frantic search for a friend to ask him if he could stand in for my hearse driver. I visited Eddie in hospital to find him quite well but rather pale and very worried, it was a shame to not be taking him.

Now, Graham is a creature of habit and is never in when you telephone, however, on a Sunday lunchtime he could be found in one of many pubs in the East End of London, the search was long but not tiresome. I left messages with all that knew him but tracked him down before closing time. To my great relief, he agreed to come and I managed to persuade him that he would not have time to use his bathing trunks even if he did take them.

The Monday morning came, it was bright though a chilly September morning, at five thirty, the inevitable pot of tea was followed by a quick check round the vehicles and we collected the family just before six and we're on our way just after. We were, of course, suited and I had given the limousine driver permission to undo his waistcoat and loosen his tie if he was hot, Graham and I were in the hearse and poor old Porky (or Steve) was all alone in the front of the limousine.

My rules on a funeral were well known, no smoking where you could normally be seen by a mourner. This allowed a quick dash round the back of the crematorium during service. This, as far as we were concerned, although longer, was no exception. I had said that we would be stopping for breakfast somewhere and that I would gauge this on the fuel consumption as we went. I knew that the family smoked and that they would not mind their driver smoking either but I had failed to ask them on his behalf.

I found out later that not long after we left, they had tapped on the glass division between driver and passengers, asking if it was alright for them to smoke, he was then asked if he had a lighter and also not to put the division back up so they could all talk. Dear Steve, he waited all the way through London and half way to Reading before he asked them if they minded if he had a smoke.

We drove uneventfully through London in the cool early morning sun and the day was warming up well by the time we reached the motorway going west. The normal speed for a funeral was between eighteen and twenty miles per hour so Graham was a little surprised when on reaching the motorway, I said "Maintain seventy." Similar surprise was evident on the faces of many truck drivers as we glid silently past.

The morning was warming up well as we enjoyed the ups and downs of Berkshire, Wiltshire and Somerset. Here and there, a hint of autumn was appearing in the foliage lining our route, Porky was still behind and making faces at me every time I looked round. Our carriageway was empty compared with the London bound commuter traffic steadily building up on the other side.

We arrived at the service station just before the Severn bridge in good time, had a break for breakfast and a stretch of the legs before we were on our way into the wilds of Wales. Then the trouble began, it all started with the hearse not pulling as well as it had been and slowly more and more up the hills, we were still in good time and at about 11 o'clock we're about sixty miles to go to catch the boat at three, I thought the trouble must be in the fuel system and we stopped in a convenient pub car park to investigate.

The family were happy to have a walk about and a drink as Graham and I took the fuel system apart to look for dirt or other foreign materials that could have caused the in loss of power. We were still not satisfied that we had found the problem when we moved on. Slowly but surely it began to get worse, it was taking us longer and longer to get up the hills, the hills were getting steeper and the time was creeping by.

It was about half-past one and we still had twenty-five miles to go, the booking in time was at two fifteen and we were crawling up hills at less than ten miles per hour. We kept telling ourselves that it was still going and breathing a sigh of relief every time we came to the brow of a hill. One good thing was that there were no traffic hold ups in front of us, however, there was, for some reason a very, very long queue behind us, we satisfied ourselves that were had no interest in the expressions on the faces of the drivers in the queue or the state of their nerves.

At long last, the road ceased its relentless journey skyward and began to make its way down to the sea, we breathed again. "I can see the sea!" we both said, followed by a silly argument of who saw it first.

Green hills and trees changed to asphalt and metal posts of the town. The old town was probably once very pretty but I had my own worries, we had come so far but there was quite a journey on the other side of the sea crossing.

We arrived at the port just about on time and presented our tickets. The hearse had to go through customs so I told Porky to wait where he was with the limousine and we would return. Now the customs shed at this port is virtually adjacent to the booking hall. However, the journey between the two took us halfway around the dock. We arrived at the required place on the other side of the building from where we had started.

Armed with a sheaf of paperwork, I entered the office where several uniformed gentlemen looked up in amazement to see a suited man in front of them, they were obviously more used to more casually dressed truck drivers. I presented the papers. Having driven the hearse into the enclosed custom shed, I was ready for an inspection and questions about the toolbox and other 'et ceteras'. I had expected a slightly more than casual approach I received, especially since we were carrying not just one but two 'pre buried' beings.

"Human remains, eh?" he glanced over in the direction of where the hearse was parked, smiled and handed the papers back and seemed totally satisfied. This seemed strange to me as not only had he not taken any copy or made any records of the passage of the remains but there was also a brick wall between where he was sitting and the hearse.

"Don't you want to see the papers for the other body?" I asked, he looked up, another man walked casually to the window and looked at the hearse.

"You've got two bodies, that's very enterprising of you. I hope you gave the customer a block rate," he said, taking about ten times the interest he had done previously, which still didn't amount much, "How did you get to do that?" he asked disinterestedly.

"Wait thirty years," I replied as casually as I thought would be acceptable. I remember from many years back that sarcasm and custom officers do not mix. The papers were handed back to me with a smile and off we went back to Porky, the limousine and her passengers.

The dear little fellah was having a conversation with a dock official who was trying to get him to move the car somewhere. There was pointing and gesticulation on behalf of the dock employee and a very emphatic "NO" emanating from my own employee. One of the greatest attributes of our dear Porky had was that if he was told to do nothing, that is precisely what he would do, interspersed with the odd cigarette. The next problem would be to reverse that order.

A cheery smile greeted our return with yards of gleaming teeth from Steve, I asked the dock official, who was by now nearing the end of his patience, where he wanted us to go. In very loud and certain terms, he told me that they were waiting to load us and that we were holding everything up. We left him almost speechless as I calmly agreed, thanked him and went back to the hearse to carry out his bidding without further ado.

I made a telephone call back to my office in London to arrange for the undertaker from Waterford to meet us with his hearse at Rosslare to take some of the load off our hearse for the next stage of the journey by road. It was with great relief that we boarded the ship and made our way to the bar for a much earned drink. It was, of course, closed until we left port.

The family was all well and not too stiff from the long journey and I apologised for the slow progress of the latter part of the journey. They were not a bit concerned, I told them what I had arranged and they all said that they were sure I had it all under control. So did I.

The weather continued to be warm, dry and pleasant for the entire four hour crossing. We all rested, drank a few beers and ate something as memorable as airline chicken and did the other exciting things that one does on ferries. It was a little colder and greyer as we arrived in the Irish port but I was very glad to see a hearse waiting for us on the dockside.

We had spoken several times on the telephone but on meeting in person, we decided to dispense with the formal titles and get straight to the first name terms.

"Hello Mr Moss, welcome to Ireland. Call me Pat. This is my son Pat and to save any confusion, we call the driver of Paddy."

"Thank you for meeting us. We had a little problem with the hearse, I'm Julian. Please meet Graham and Porky," I said.

"Er, excuse me Mr Moss," interjected our little fat friend, "Could we please dispense with the 'Porky' this once as I am trying very hard to lose weight and we are only here for two days and I wouldn't want to seem too familiar."

"Oh, sorry Porks, how thoughtless of me," I agreed. "Pat, this is 'CT', it's short for Cuddly Toy."

"Er, excuse me Mr Moss, not that name, the one before that, if you don't mind." He put his hand up to his mouth and whispered loudly behind it, "Stephen."

"Oh, I thought you just used that for tax purposes, not be uttered in public."

With the introductions over and with funereally straight faces, we took the heavier coffin from our hearse and transferred it into theirs and set off. Our hearse was certainly not a hundred per cent but it was a great deal better. Slowly, the grey evening gave way to the black of a country night as we travelled the forty or so miles to the beautiful little town of Waterford.

We stopped briefly outside the hotel at the dockside and the limousine was unloaded whilst the two hearses made a quick exit to the undertaker's garage for the night, followed closely by the limousine. I am sure that it was a very picturesque sight with the street lamps shining on the fishing boats tied up at the dock but it was now pouring with rain and we were all dashing for cover.

I booked us all into our rooms. I quickly changed my suit and tie to look less funeral and made my way to the undertaker's garage to clarify the arrangements for the following day. The outlining of this took but a few minutes and as the time was getting late, we made haste for the dining room at the hotel to eat before last call.

This undertaking business is thirsty work and, after all, we were in Ireland so there was Guinness to sample. A few pints later, we were all ready to hit the hay; we had had a long day and the next two days would be just as tiring.

The next morning was bright and sunny although with a chill in the air, we, the staff rose early and made our way to the garage to wash the cars. I had a good look around the hearse's engine and spent a good hour working on it to try and find its problem, but nothing was obvious. We just had time for breakfast before the service was to take place. We were meeting the family at the cathedral.

Washed, changed and fed, we made for Pat's garage, checked that all was ready. "Cigarettes out!—and you Porky."

"Stephen, call me Stephen, just for today, that's all I ask and then I shall return to my usual position under a stone." He muttered as he walked to his gleaming limousine.

"Sorry, Porks."

I stopped the traffic in the main street that ran down to the cathedral and ushered the cars past me, the limousine came by. "Sorry, sir, I don't know what came over me this near to payday, please feel free to call me anything you like."

These 'asides' used to take place at all times, usually directed in a whisper to the intended recipient with a totally deadpan face, some were so funny that keeping a straight face was a matter of firmly biting the inside of your cheeks and trying not to look any of the staff directly in the face.

We arrived at the cathedral, a large crowd had arrived for the mass and were making their way inside whilst the family were waiting to follow in behind the two coffins. The clergy appeared in their splendid gowns, I introduced them to the family.

The coffins were blessed and purified in the normal way, with bearers ducking the deluge. It must be the same the world over and the procession made its way into the cathedral.

I had been too late the previous evening to take a look inside the cathedral as I would have liked to in order to know the layout and mentally plan appropriate seating for the family. Getting this wrong can look very odd. Any priest, vicar or preacher will have a favourite side of the church from which to conduct a service and these vary. Sometimes, they will preach from the lectern and sometimes not. It looks wrong with the relatives sat on one side and the priest preaching on the empty other side. I began to usher the family to what looked the correct side, a cough attracted my attention. It was Pat, thumb firmly indicating the other side of the cathedral.

"Would you like to take the front row in this side?" I whispered to Teresa and the family, changing direction in mid-flow. *Thanks Pat*, I winked.

All the staff were now lined up to bow before leaving the church.

At the back of the cathedral, the local staff took to their pews for the mass, I took my lot, of similar creed to myself, well outside the building, I thought that we had had enough to go wrong so far without risking divine retribution.

The cathedral, as with any Basilica, was beautifully decorated inside, the frescoes and statues were fantastic and the proportions of the overall effect of actually being inside this building made one feel very small. There were beautifully carved wooden and marble pieces, the lighting and the frescoes were subtle but full. It was a beautiful place.

The passersby were interested by the fact that there were not only two hearses outside but also by the fact that there were strange cars in the area. My two Royces always blended in well with other funeral cars, rather like the Queen Mary would blend in with a rowing boat. "Did you come all the way from England?" and "Is this the funeral from London?" were the questions of the day as we stood outside the church in the sun.

A careful eye on the watch told me that the service was going to end soon, a glance inside reflected the same. The fingers went up outside, one, three, four or five to indicate the number of minutes to the end of the service. The boys came in and we positioned ourselves silently at the sides of the church to be ready at the end of the service.

We proceeded out of the church, loaded the hearses with the inevitable avoidance of drowning, ushered the mourners to the car and set off to the cemetery.

The distance was farther than I had envisaged. However, we arrived in less than twenty minutes at this beautiful spot on the edge of a little valley overlooking a river lazily winding its way seaward. It was certainly different to take a funeral through winding country lanes and have to wait whilst harvesting machinery and tractors went about their labours rather than the red buses and juggernauts I was used to. The order of interment at the cemetery was the same as before with dad going in first covered by the required amount of earth before Mum was placed to rest again, the committal was said and we left the graveside quietly and took the family back to the hotel.

We allowed the cemetery staff plenty of time to fill in the grave and our next job was to go back in the afternoon to set up the memorial so we had lunch. I arranged with the family to take them back to the grave to see the stone set in place at 5 o'clock.

Discussions with the local undertaker about the cost of his services delayed our meal and still I could not make him state his price, very difficult. We finally came to a figure and I paid the man his dues. Our ideas of lunch varied immensely, he suggested the local restaurant when I was thinking of a pie and a pint and back to work. We had a quick lunch in the restaurant and dashed off to the cemetery in the limousine, with three of us up front and all the memorials in the boot.

Nearing the cemetery, we passed through the same little village we had that morning, a sleepy little place with no pavements, single story white buildings with contrasting slate roofs and town planning that could only be described as 'random' resulting in the main road through the village being the nearest thing to a straight line without running into any of the houses.

In the middle of the main street, an old dog lay in the road, as we approached, an ear twitched and set itself in the direction of arrival, slowly followed by the raising of the nose bringing the eyes to focus in our general direction. It was obvious that this was a busy thoroughfare. Reluctantly, the beast rose and meandered to the side of the road, exhausted by this unplanned exercise, he flopped down to continue his interrupted day's labours. We continued on to the cemetery to smile and wave from all the passer-by.

We drove up the hill out of the village, the green pasture land sloping from our right, down to the river valley now some distance off to our left.

"It's turn right somewhere up here, isn't it?" I said.

"I wasn't really watching this morning but I don't remember it being this far!" said Graham.

"Well," said Porky, "we could always go back to the village and ask the throng that lined our route."

"Don't be daft," barked Graham, "he's probably gone home by now."

"Well, maybe there is a pub in the village," said Porks cheerily.

"I bet there is but we have to put this memorial up," I replied.

"I meant that we could always ask at the pub," said Steve in an informative way, "Oh no, maybe not," he changed his tone, "when have any of us lot been able to leave before closing time close!"

We took the next right since it looked familiar. It happily led into the lane with the cemetery at the end.

It was a sunny afternoon in this tiny dry stone walled cemetery. The gravediggers had long since gone, leaving a tidy though uneven mound where we had buried that morning. We levelled the area at the head of the grave and set the base for the headstone on solid ground. It is important to have this base perfectly level so that the headstone would stand perfectly upright from the start, since a lean in any direction will only increase in time.

Cutting away soil from the high part was my job, laying the base in place went to Porky whilst Graham, being the heaviest was acting as pile driver to effect the tamping down and fine adjustments in an attempt to make the bubble stay in the centre of the spirit level. After a few attempts, we even had sound effects emanating from the pile driver. There were naturally the helpful hints and observations.

"Here, that bubble has moved to the other end now. You've got the spirit levelled the wrong way round." And "Let me understand this, we want the bubble in the middle so why don't we let some of the fluid out of the other end of that tube and then the bubble will have to move up."

These helpful hints were all I was going to get, as usual, from this sarcastic lot. "Have you been at the embalming fluid again?"

Several attempts were made before the bubble rested in the centre for both axes.

"Now you've got it to stay there why don't you hold it in place with this nail!" was the next suggestion. I should have left both of them in the pub.

We set up the headstone with flower vases at each side, conveniently covering the holes that had been previously used to secure the side kerbs from the full size memorial back in England. The bible was set up and stuck together in the centre of the grave then all parts were cleaned down removing any little marks that had occurred in transit, with a final tidy up, the whole job was done in under two hours in spite of the helpful hints.

I often wonder what anyone passing by would have thought about our inane banter with its cartoon like logic, over-exaggerated mannerisms and deadpan deliveries. It went on just the same before we had the embalming fluid in the workshops so we couldn't blame that!

Now we come to the sad part. With all traces of rubbish removed from the cemetery and tools, buckets, water containers, and trolleys loaded, we left. I did not know until we arrived back in England that we were driving leaving my favourite hammer all alone in the cemetery. We had worked together for over ten years and this had been our fifth country together.

Unaware of my now lost companion, we drove back toward the village, there was a certain licking and smacking of lips emanating from the crew.

"Wassa time John?" asked Graham, everyone in the east of London is known as 'John' at these times.

"Bout arf past, I would say," said Porks. Nobody was in the least interested at half past what as we drove into the village. The dog had placed itself back in the centre of the road, an ear focused in our direction. This was obviously too much for one day, he eased himself up with his forelegs and had a good scratch before letting us pass.

"Then we're late then!" said Graham, studying the village intently. "Aha!" A huge fist shot in front of my nose with index finger outstretched.

"If I am not mistaken," he said eloquently, "that," the finger rotated and reaffirmed its direction, "is what passes, in this very green and ridiculously expensive land, as a BOOZER."

I was outvoted two to one, but not for long, as the boss, I cast my deciding vote. We stopped.

It would seem that the vast majority of undertakers drink and some have been known to exceed the medically recommended daily intake on more than one evening of the week. It could be the job that has its difficulties with unpleasant sights and smells that bring a man to drink in order to dull the senses of smell and memory of the horrors but I think not.

I am of the opinion that as very few people actually want the job, the thinking drinker uses this as a damn good excuse to have a drink whenever he wants. The liberal scattering of few choice comments, such as "Listen, if you had just been and collected what I have, your stomach would have thrown your dinner a world record-breaking distance and now I'm trying to have a quiet drink. OK?" has always had the desired effect.

Graham and the CT took another vote and decided on the designated driver.

"And it's no good trying that 'deciding vote' stuff again. You've already used it once today. Anyway, you still have to collect the family and take them back to the gravesite to see the stone, sir." It could often be like a kindergarten.

They had quite a few beers, chatted up the barmaid relentlessly and continued the usual inane conversation, much to the amusement of others, with a beer in hand, these two were a great deal of fun.

Graham had several ways of winding up Steve at these times, he would say condescending things like "Bless his little heart!" and "Oh look at his little face." Which would bring all sorts of replies from our Porky such as "Absolutely no manners, butting in like that!" and "Excuse me, sir—Shut it!" all this would be delivered with the usual deadpan expression and no malice. Everything was always expressed with the utmost politeness and there were never any swearwords used or offence given to anyone.

The time flew by and we had to leave. I changed and met the family for whom lunch had slipped pleasantly into teatime. They had caught up with some old friends of their parents and found a great deal to chat over. I met the boys at the bar and the ladies sitting not far away. When they were ready, we left.

Since leaving Clapton the previous morning, I had not had much contact with the family, what with mechanical problems and last-minute arrangements. I was very pleased to see them in such good spirits as we drove to the cemetery once more. I took pictures of them beside the grave and of the sun setting on the far side of the river. They were visibly moved by the fact that their wishes had now been carried out and expressed their gratitude with both tears and embraces, it was a very emotional occasion. We stayed there for some considerable length of time.

I took the car back to the garage after dropping the family at the hotel, we had discussed the return journey, which was to start at 6 o'clock the next morning. When I walked back to the hotel, I found my two drivers at the bar, surprise-surprise and a beer awaiting my arrival, compliments of the family. With the car safely in the garage until the morning, I had some catching up to do.

We spent an hour with the family before taking our leave for dinner, followed by some time in appreciation of the fineness of real Irish Guinness before hitting the hay.

It was a waste of time trying to catch up with these experts but I did make a good account of myself.

Tea and toast arrived at five fifteen in the morning, the three of us had been sharing a room. I had a shower and a loud chorus of 'Jerusalem' hoping to rouse the other two, Graham was first up but dear little Porks was true to form with just a grunt. I went to pay the bill and make sure that the family was up. They had not been delivered their tea so reparations were made in the lobby. Cars were brought and we set off at about a quarter past six, not bad. Without the extra weight, the hearse was behaving much better but not perfect so we paced our journey gently to Rosslare.

In the dark of our outward journey, we had not had time to appreciate the little villages we had passed through with the odd glimpse of the sea to the south. One fishing village I had remembered from the outward journey was just like a picture postcard in daylight and without the rain. Its stone houses and fishing boats alongside the dock, all painted in bright colours, surrounded on three sides with green hills, belied the awful weather so common to this Atlantic coast.

The countryside and gently rolling hills gave way to the outskirts of the town and we descended to the dock, following the inevitable signs to 'CAR FERRY'. The route followed by these signs always seemed to take in all the best views of industrial parks, railway sidings and the roughest road surfaces, whilst the most direct way is to drive straight through the town but nobody ever has the nerve to try it.

The 'CAR FERRY' signs ceased and we were confronted with a large official looking sign that stated firmly 'WAIT HERE'. We waited obediently in the middle of nowhere. The most unlikely looking official appeared from a little hut and beckoned us over. We triumphantly passed the sign and drove toward the hut where the man in wellies, trousers too large and jacket too tight over his thick jumper, told us that he had not meant us to bring the cars, just the tickets.

Happily, he ushered us to an area and told us that we would be first on the boat when they loaded. This was fine since, at the time, we were the only people on the dock and being last on, would still have put us at the front.

For the next hour, we all sat in, wandered around and generally leant against the cars in the cold, grey crisp morning until we were told to drive on. Everyone jumped back into the car and we drove on to the ferry taking "pole position" for that "off" at the other end, we were about the first people onto the passenger decks. I only saw the family once during this crossing and I do not know where they went to.

Unusually, our Steve went straight to the canteen and the magnetic smell of cooking breakfast. I refrained from using the word 'cannibal', as he stood solitarily at the front of a line at the closed buffet, Graham and I went walkabout. The bar and coffee shop were both closed so we returned to the canteen and our Porks.

At that precise moment, we saw the canteen open and made haste to join our little friend at the front of the now lengthy queue, being in a good mood, I let the other two fall in behind me, another advantage of being the boss, being outwitted again, they let me pay. Well, I did get them up very early. We now had the choice of places to sit in the restaurant.

We took our places in a line with our backs to the canteen and the door to the deck on our left and set about breakfast. It was not long before the tables began to fill up.

In front of our trio sat a couple from the United States of America, we all nodded in a friendly way as they came to the table. I was seated at the right-hand end of the table with Graham to my left and Steve on his left. We chatted to the American pair and discovered that they had been travelling through the British Isles and were now on their way back to England for their journey back to Louisiana. There was a lull in the conversation as we neared the end of our breakfast. Graham was the first to break the silence.

"Times getting on 'Skip'," he said, looking at his watch.

"OK Chief, can I finish my breakfast? We've got a good tide running," I replied with more than a little pique in my tone.

The lady from Louisiana looked up at the suited gents in front of them. "Oh, are you the crew, I didn't think."

Graham introduced us, me as Captain, himself as Chief and Porky, "Bless his little heart!" as navigator.

"Shut it – Chief!" said Porks on cue, followed by a polite, "Sorry madam" across the table.

We did not really expect anyone to believe a word but they took it all in and asked us all how long we have been doing this job, the answers were duly given, but we did fail to mention that we had been undertakers for that length of time.

"Come on fellas, we are two minutes from the off," I butted it in.

We all wiped our mouths with our napkins, folded them, dropped them on that table and rose together, marching off, bidding our leave from our new-found friends with Porky holding the door for Graham and me as we walked toward the bridge deck. "I know I'm the lowest of the low and expected to open the door for you but a 'Thank you' wouldn't harm would it now, Sir," Steve said in his usual loud sarcastic manner.

"He only does it for the sympathy of the passengers," Graham said to me unemotionally as he hurried along behind us.

Two minutes had not elapsed before the ship shuddered into motion, we wondered whether our breakfast companions were taken in.

Sometime later and after we had found our way to the bar, we discovered that we had, indeed, taken our friends truly for a ride as their faces now showed their disbelief at our not being at our supposed posts.

As we neared the shores of Wales, we had a quick sandwich to fortify us for the long journey home, met the family and agreed to meet at the cars before disembarkation.

Since the hearse was not well, it was decided that the limousine would go ahead with the family and that I would follow with the hearse fending for myself as I went, though it reminded me of being left on the Great Cambridge Road some ten years before, they did have a point. Firstly, it was my car, secondly, they were just hired help, thirdly, if anyone could fix it on the road, I could and lastly and by no means least, they would just arrive in London in time for the pubs to open and if the hearse broke down, they might not get a drink that evening. I waved them goodbye with a smile.

I filled the hearse up with petrol and began my slow journey back with a smile. I had not reached the outskirts of Fishguard before I saw our little fat friend frantically waving at me from the road outside a petrol station. I pulled in and paid for their fuel as they waved another goodbye. "Friends of yours?" said the garage proprietor sarcastically.

It was yet another fine hot day as I made my way slowly up the hills and quickly down them, I was maintaining quite good speeds through the green Welsh countryside. At the beginning of the motorway, I stopped at the services for a break and a drink of water. As I drove into the entry ramp of the services, the limousine was coming the other way. I received smiles and waves from all the occupants before I watched the car effortlessly take its place in the fast lane before disappearing over the hill.

After I had cooled down and had a drink, I returned to the hearse still wearing my three-piece suit with striped trousers. There were three men wandering around the car. It is unusual to see a hearse parked in a motorway service station, they spotted me as I approached.

"Is this your car, then?" asked one.

"Yes!" I replied, thinking that the first guess was good but knowing that the next thing they said would either be less interesting or downright stupid.

"Are you an undertaker, then?" I could not decide into which category this fell.

"No," I said, never expecting them to believe me.

"Oh, what do you do then?" came next.

"You mean what am I doing in a service station in Wales in a 1958 Rolls Royce hearse?" I thought I would get them on the run.

"Yes, you don't see many of these around."

"I collect and restore them." This sort of reply is not really meant to be misleading but I tended to avoid conversations about the job more and more than once you admit you're an undertaker you become the butt of all the bad taste humour that must have first been translated from the tombs of the Valley of the Kings by Howard Carter. Striking doubt into inquiring minds at the first instance was always fun and I never ceased to be amazed what people would actually believe would only be the slightest ring of truth.

"Well, you're certainly dressed like an undertaker!" at this point some quick thinking was required, he did have a point, my mind was racing. I leant inside the car and popped the bonnet catch to check the levels before I went and to give me some time.

"I always wear the uniform for the job. It saves the stupid questions!" Blank looks, great, I had won. The levels were fine, I locked the bonnet down. I continued.

"If I had been wearing a tee shirt, jeans and sneakers, you would have taught it very odd me walking up to this car so how would you think any police patrol would view the situation. It makes long distances easier and less interrupted." Even I believed it.

They all agreed that they had never thought of it in that way and decided that I was a very smart man indeed. The car started with a little swish of the starter and I began my silent departure.

"Bye, lads," I waved, thinking that there had been three born in the same minute.

A broad grin spread across my face as I left, this degenerated into uncontrollable laughter as the hearse and I slid silently onto the motorway together, much to the interest of the occupants of passing cars.

The motorway was fairly busy for a Wednesday and I spent most of the journey in the slow lane at about fifty miles per hour taking turns to play 'leapfrog' as I passed the heavy trucks uphill and they came thundering past on the downgrades. The industrial areas of Port Talbot passed and the road became busier still as it snaked its way toward the capital. The green hills of Wales are fairly gentle in the south alongside this road and the feint smell of the ocean is always in the southerly breeze.

The job was now over, the family were safely on their way home and I was taking the lame duck home, gauges were normal and though travelling a little slowly for a Rolls, I realised that for the first time since I had received the confirmation from the Home Office, I had nothing else to think about than enjoying the drive home.

Swishing silently along, I remembered the famous road test of the Silver Cloud in 'Motor' magazine over thirty years before. "The loudest sound that can be heard at sixty miles per hour in this car is the ticking of the clock!"

I was very glad that this had broken several years before, as I hadn't brought my ear defenders. I was keeping a count of the miles travelled against time and I was returning about forty-five miles per hour on average, which would get me to London at about eight that evening.

Something unusual attracted my attention in the rearview mirror, there was a large truck behind me and another slowly gaining on me in the next lane out and in between the two, the unmistakable curve of the rear wing of the Phantom limousine, I had not long passed another service station and therefore surmised that the others had pulled in there for a break. Knowing that Graham would have most certainly seen me, I wondered what evil little plan he could be hatching, otherwise he would have been going at least twenty miles per hour faster.

As the gradient of the hill increased the trucks slowed and I began to pull ahead, the limousine overtook the truck and pulled alongside me, I expected the worst, something wet, at least. I looked round with a smile. Thumbs up from them was returned as thumbs up OK! I waved them to go on. The exhaust note changed almost imperceptibly as this two and a half ton monster pulled ahead as if moving off from a standstill, a couple of minutes later it was out of sight.

I found out later that they had hung back behind me for some time whilst trying to think up a trick to play on me but decided against it since they had passengers on board and didn't want to alarm them.

The Severn bridge was not too crowded and now we were back in England with about one hundred and twenty miles to go, gauges normal and all's well.

I arrived at the outskirts of London at eight as the sun was sinking low in the West, thankful to be this near home, I wondered what the traffic would be like through the centre and how the 'old girl' would handle it in her unhappy state. Happily, my fears were unfounded and I arrived back in Clapton just a few minutes before nine. The limousine had not been back for many minutes as they had decided to take a different route through London and had not been as lucky as me with the traffic.

Thankful that it was now all over and job done well, with all involved satisfied, there was only one thing left to do after we had parked the cars.

LAST ONE THERE BUYS THE BEER!

Chapter Nine
A Funny Thing That Happened to Me on the Way to the Crematorium

Large families are now not as common as they were sixty or so years ago; six or more siblings were quite common and so, tragically, were the number of infant mortalities. These large families will tend all to get married within a few years of each other, have their children within the same few years and naturally died within a similar timespan.

Many times have I overheard a conversation at a funeral when the most salient line would be. "Do you remember, it wasn't that long ago when we all used to meet at weddings and christenings, now it only seems to be funerals."

It was not unusual, therefore, to meet the same family several times over a period of five or six years and thus, get to know them very well by sight, if not by name. It was the women with whom I would make the most contact, firstly, they would make the arrangements and secondly, I would see and meet them as they were going about their normal daily shopping in the area. The contact would range from a recognising nod to stopping for a chat lasting five minutes or more. The other people to get on good terms weight naturally, were the staff at Old People's Homes.

With luck, from the business point of view, getting involved with the family at the first loss and creating a good impression was of the utmost importance. One Sunday evening, the telephone rang, "Is that Hawes, the undertaker?"

I intimated that this was indeed the undertakers and gently ushered the lady's thinking around to the fact that this was not the "Hawes the undertakers" but "Mosses, THE UNDERTAKERS," a slight slip of the phone directory had turned in our favour. A few quiet words later and we were on our way to the Old People's Home to collect a body. Usual thing, well maintained, present owner has no further use for! The funeral was duly arranged and carried out.

Unbeknown to me, I had made quite an impression on the matron of the home and was quite surprised to receive a call from the coroner's officer late one evening some months later to remove the remains of a person who had died on the estate well off our patch.

"You know the sister, apparently," said Ray, the coroner's man. "I dunno, we can't keep up with you single guys, you will use any angle for a job," he joked.

We were to collect the brother of the matron of the Home who had died at his own home. As I have mentioned, the relationship with the coroner's officer is one of the most important things to a funeral director, Ray and I had made firm friends from the time we met and I had laughed at his jokes about his wife's cooking. When I met Janet sometime later, I found her to be a wonderful cook and I have her permission to say so, even if she is taller than me!

Ray warned me that the removal that we were about to embark on was for an extremely large gent and that the brothers would be there to help and we would have to collect the keys for the flat from the police station.

Now collecting keys from police stations fell into two categories. The first was, "Give us the keys to the mortuary, John!" which might solicit such a request as "What for?" from the officer on duty, followed by the man in the suit saying, "I'm not feeling well and I think I ought to lie down."

This would usually work because I think they are taught in police school that policemen can only ever be trained to a level of sarcasm which equals less than ten per cent of that of a trainee undertaker. On those occasions when this was insufficient, one could be hit with, "Got any I.D.?"

You never had since you had just given your last and dog-eared business card to the relatives. This meant that stronger tactics were called for, "Do you want to come and have a sniff in the back of my van, little boy?" always worked. This would result in being given the keys to the mortuary when we could go in and steal anybody we wanted to.

The second case was when the keys requested were for a residence where someone had died, this was altogether different.

"Got the keys of 55, Rathbone Court, John?" you always started with something at least familiar.

"I'm busy, wait your turn outside," the officer would say. The undertaker would now attempt to attract the attention of another officer at the back of the front office, gesticulating, 'KEYS' and 'dead things' or people asleep.

"I thought I asked you to wait outside. I'm dealing with this gentleman," the front desk man would say.

I then whisper quietly to the officer, "Well look, I'm want the keys to number 55, Rathbone Court and the keys to the mortuary, to save me a trip and I didn't want to come in here and announce the fact as you may well be dealing with some distressed relative at this very moment, also I have no particular wish to wait half an hour outside in line, just to get the keys."

"Oh, OK," said the officer, understanding. Turning to one of his colleagues behind and shouting. "It's the undertaker come for the keys for the stiff on the Pendleton estate, somebody sort him out." So much for tact and subtlety.

Eventually, someone would arrive with keys and the inevitable form. The paperwork would be thrust under one's nose for completion.

"Name, address, date of birth, occupation, height, weight, telephone number and shoe size!" I scribbled away and returned the form, only wanting to take the keys away for an hour.

The officer studies the form, Richard Frederick Conway, 55, Rathbone Court, Pendleton Estate followed by a lot of blanks.

"I can let you have the other information later but I don't think I will be able to get you a signature. Now can I have the keys, please?" I said innocently.

The officer, totally dumbfounded at the blank innocent expression that confronted him, obviously remembered his training and the bit about undertakers sarcasm, signs the form himself and hands me the keys.

"Can I have the mortuary keys as well, please?"

Silently, the officer thrust the extra set of keys under my nose with one hand whilst pulling at his hair with the other. I've always wondered why there are so many bald policemen.

With armfuls of keys, we were on our way, Frank and I.

"I used to live on this estate," said Frank, driving into a blocked entrance. "It wasn't like this when I lived here," he said, backing out into the road again.

We eventually found the correct block and then tried to sort out the numbers. Some of the blocks on estates are numbered logically so that the mail delivery can start at number one and proceed through to the highest number without having to retrace their steps, some are numbered on a logical one to seven, ground floor, eight to fourteen on the first and so on, others are detailed by unemployed bingo callers and there must be a great number of them. Tired and harassed, we found the apartment. I wondered whether the policeman had a worse sense of humour than me, but the keys did work and in we went.

A giant of a creature lay on the single bed in the spartan apartment, empty tobacco tins formed piles from floor to ceiling three times and a few less spectacular piles played supporting roles. Frank and I looked at each other, aware of our recent surgeries, his back and my shoulder, we stood there. This mountain of a man we estimated at about twenty-four stone or more and judging by the overhang at the end of the bed was certainly nearly six foot six.

"Well," said Frank, "he won't move on his own."

"We could always pray," I said, "you're the religious one, get to it."

"Sarcasm will get you nowhere."

"It got me here with you," I said before I had realised that this would not achieve anything.

We had the stretcher and laid this out on the floor and installed the remains therein with the least possible bump, we had swung the bed round in the room to give us plenty of elbow room so that neither of us would be struggling near to the wall at the head of the bed. Now we wrapped the covers of the stretcher over the body and tightened the straps to stop him from moving.

We stood and looked some more. Again, this produced nothing. We were as ready as we would be at any time of day or night between periods "A" and "C" (see chapter one). This was it.

There was no going back. No time like the present. "I'm ready if you are!" this was an obvious lie.

One, two, three—four, five, six. Nice day for it. A nod is as good as a wink to, a blind horse! Still nothing. There was only one thing for it.

"You' ready, Frank?"

"I was waiting for you. You're the boss!"

"Does that mean that I decide when to go?" I asked.

"Of course it does, Silly," he said in a childish manner.

"Well then, let's go," I said, walking past the body toward the door.

"Julian," he said, hands on his hips.

"We have got to take this with us," pointing downward.

"But you said that I was the boss, didn't you?"

"Yes."

"Then, I decide what to do, right?"

"Yes."

"So, if I think that we are lacking in brain cells to attempt to move this body, then that's my job, as boss, right!"

"Well, I suppose so, but if we don't move it, we don't get paid for it."

"Why didn't you say so?" I said, walking back and picking up my end. A different light had been put on the matter.

We stood there with this huge weight strung between us and shuffled toward the doorway, arms getting more primate, like every inch of the way. We were out of the bedroom and in the corridor between the kitchen and bathroom, where we stopped for a rest.

We had some way to go, which included four half flights of stairs, there was no lift, naturally.

"It'll be easier when we get to the stairs," said Frank as we rested. This was quite correct, since the stretcher would slide on the stairs as we restrained it.

"Damn good job we live above ground and now below, would be worse trying to drag people upstairs when the lift didn't work," I thought out loud.

We braced ourselves for the next haul and picked up our respective ends, we had just stood upright and were ready to move when two of the wooden slats that were the backbone of the stretcher broke. This made the whole thing uneven in balance and it started to tip over in our hands. Instinctively we put the ends down before falling.

We stood in the hallway, looking at our problem, knowing that it would not go away. The problem now was that the remaining slats had very little chance of holding the weight, even if we were to try. This was the precise moment that the sister chose to appear in the doorway. We told her of the problem and that we were probably going to have to get another man to complete the job but not to worry. Being a very practical Irish woman, she understood the problem completely and told us that her brothers would be there in a minute and that they would be only too pleased to help.

The boys arrived and were, indeed, very willing. We still had to struggle our way down the stairs into the van and were suitably worn out when we had finished.

Unloading at the mortuary was also entertaining but we managed to borrow an unsuspecting policeman from the police station on our way. I sent Frank in this time, when he returned with an officer after a few minutes, I was suitably impressed until the officer expressed surprise in finding me as he got into the van.

"I thought you said you were on your own," he turned to Frank.

"I did, but if I had told you that we had about twenty-five stone of remains, would you have volunteered?" as he ushered the duped bobby firmly into the front seat, he was by now firmly trapped between the two of us. At least he saw the funny side and gave his best effort to get the job done with a minimum of fuss so we counted ourselves very lucky.

When the time came for the funeral, the brothers were insistent that they would carry the casket, notwithstanding the peels of opposition from my eager staff, who had been looking forward to the crushed vertebrae and torn muscles with their usual sarcasm. They all promised faithfully to attend church daily for the remainder of their days.

The brothers did an admirable job in carrying their brother, both in and out of church and to the graveside at the cemetery. With the added attraction that one of the brothers owned a public house, we all agreed that this was a very worthwhile family to impress from 'Day One'.

Stories that one hears are just as interesting as things that happen in front of one's very eyes.

We were involved with the funeral of a West Indian woman who had reached the wonderful age of 103 years, by the number of family involved with the arranging and the incessant flow of visitors to our chapel, this had been one very popular lady indeed. Luckily, we had a very good spot at the cemetery and the immediate families were very pleased with all we had done. I was therefore pleased at having been able to carry out everything to their satisfaction and what with our luck of having excellent weather, I knew that the recommendation of our name had a good chance of spreading over a wide area over the coming years.

The grandson came up to me and thanked me for all my efforts and as we talked, he unfolded this wonderful story. The woman was purported to be the oldest West Indian resident of the United Kingdom and had been very proud of the fact, she had received her telegram from the Queen on her 100th birthday and had never ceased to wave this at all who came to her door, she'd also been proud to be a British Citizen but it was within this fact that an intriguing story lay.

Her sister, Sylvia, who was three years younger, had emigrated to Britain many years before, was living here and did not like it. In the late fifties, Victoria had been in the Caribbean and wanted to come here. The simple trip of Sylvia home followed by Victoria's entry into the country had gone without a hitch. The two old ladies had thought this their wicked little secret and had giggled incessantly at their own devilment. The result had, of course, been that the lady we had buried at the ripe old age of 103 had actually been a full three years older at a fantastic 106 years of age.

Another time worth mention purely for its reasons of apparent compassion, was when I was arranging the funeral of a woman who had died in her fifties, leaving four daughters all under the age of about thirty. The difficulty in dealing with this distressed quartet and their husbands/boyfriends were apparent from the beginning.

Being in my mid-thirties, I was not so hardened that I was not aware of their problems and grief. This served to remind me that I would, one day, lose my own parents and have to deal with that eventuality, probably alone. I therefore felt involved. There was a great deal of coming and going for the arrangements, with a multitude of questions from all sides of the family.

The funeral had been arranged to start from their home with about four limousines in tow. It was April with its associated showers and this particular day was the quintessence of April in England. The staff were fed up because they would have to wash the cars first thing in the morning as usual, they would probably get filthy. The order to "Get that lot cleaned up before we go out this afternoon," which was always met with shrieks of pleasure.

We had to reverse into the cul-de-sac to start the funeral and I had allowed plenty of time for this since it was long, twisty and always full of cars. The day had started off sunny and thus the cars had had to be presented 'squeaky clean'. The moment we had ventured out of the garage, the heavens had opened and soaked the cars, leaving them dripping.

We had been lucky insofar as the cars had not yet started to show the dirt that they would do so soon, as they dried, being black. I was looking to impress this family with a slick, smart turnout that would run from start to finish so smoothly that they would hardly be aware of our presence. DRAT!

After a long battle with hired drivers to get their cars where I wanted them, I was pleased enough with the positioning of the fleet to meet the family and discuss the loading of the flowers, this was going to be tough on the drivers since all the rules of flower ordering had been broken in every plane available, this sizes of some of the tributes were ridiculous. Everyone was in a great state of distress and this was beginning to show in their anxiety. Problems were not helped by the fact that they had assumed that I would start the funeral from the back of the house and had set the flowers out accordingly meaning that we had now to take all the floral tributes through the house to load them onto the cars.

With this mammoth task completed by the staff, very well, in view of the unexpected problems they had been presented with, we were ready to get the family set in their places in the cars. We now had a different problem that which I had become so used. A multitude of women in a very small house with only one bathroom, wishing to tidy up before leaving. They were really very quick and I had luckily allowed plenty of time for other eventualities that had not reared their heads, so my timing was near enough so far.

I had asked one of the boyfriends to compile a list of names of people to be sitting in each car and now it was my job to find him. I looked around in despair at the sea of faces until he happily found me. Armed with the boyfriend and list, we set off to 'Round up' the family, he made the job a breeze.

We were ready to go in no time. The cars were still wet but the day was drying out fast, which would result in a very grey looking 'Mishmash' that had been such proud cars only an hour earlier. The street was lined with cherry trees, which were, at this time, filled with abundant pink blossom. A major deity chose this very moment to breathe out and in our general direction causing the release of petals from the boughs in such quantity and symmetry to cover all the cars with the most beautiful panoply of pinky white scales that changed the entire soul of the funeral itself.

Everyone started crying at this transformation, even I had to search for a handkerchief with which to extract a grain of dust that the breeze had blown in my eye. The whole attitude of the job was immediately transformed, I became happy and the family followed suit.

Some things never failed to get me riled and the favourite one was when people blocked the exit or entry to or from my garage doors, especially when I had work to do. I was always amazed when local residents would say that they thought that nobody ever used this entrance as they had never ever seen it used. What on earth did they expect, the doors left open for all to walk in unannounced to a garage full of Rolls Royce with direct access to other people's deceased relatives.

Our doors were fully closed and locked at all times when they were not actually in use for transit in or out. I was also amazed by the fact that people would knock at the garage door and wait there for someone to show up as if there was an employee permanently stationed just inside the door to pander to their every whim. Really, the telephone and its associated directory has been in existence for many years now, I think it's about time that England learnt how to use it.

Many times would it happen that we would open or try to open the garage doors, to go out on a removal or funeral, to find a car parked firmly in front of the doors, thus blocking our way. When we knew whose car it was, we could easily find the culprit and get the offending vehicle removed. Strangers were a different matter altogether.

Private funeral businesses usually run on a very small funerals per year and in London, an average of 200 funerals per year seems to be considered a good number for one shop. This averages out a four per week, however, there is no such thing as average in the funeral trade. Anyone who has ever waited for a London bus will easily be able to understand the problem known officially as 'bunching'.

After waiting an hour for a service that is supposed to be ten times every hour, they all come along together. With funerals, this can make some days very busy with as many as three funerals and leave other times of about a week with very little work, if any.

Therefore, the timing of a funeral can be quite critical, especially getting in and out of the garage. Explaining this to inconsiderate parkers can be frustrating. The attitude is both thoughtless and insulting, "What's the hurry? He is dead, isn't he?" and of course, the same people would be those who would make the most fuss at being late for one of their relative's funerals.

We would normally be able to find the culprit within a few minutes so no harm done, however, one day, when we had exhausted our efforts in the usual business premises and the offending car remained stubbornly in the way, I hit upon a new idea.

Getting out the company's large trolley jack and placing it underneath the rear axle and lifting enough to clear the back wheels from the ground, we dragged the car into the middle of the street and left it there. Our cars were the first to leave the scene and as I closed the garage doors, the queue of cars waiting to get past this car, now in the middle of the road and blocking it completely, was building up nicely.

The hooters started, which I thought may attract the attention of the owners of the car, but, just in case, I called the police to inform them of this badly parked vehicle before leaving for the funeral in the opposite direction. When we returned to the garage, all was normal. We never did see that car again.

Another occasion when obstruction of the garage doors led to fret, worry and disaster for one of the floral tributes started early one morning with one of my drivers phoning up to say that he was not going to be in for work that day and, having two funerals out meant a fairly full day as both at church services.

I had managed to obtain replacement drivers at short notice from two different sources, the disadvantage of this is simply that hired drivers do not usually expect to have to wash a car. I had had to wash a car myself first thing that morning as well as attending to my other duties. The morning funeral went without a hitch. However, the cars were looking particularly grimy since the deluge that had wasted it time over our heads whilst there was a perfectly good reservoir not far away that could well have done with the water. The morning driver had taken his money and fled, the afternoon man had yet to arrive. It was again a matter of rolling up the sleeves and buckling down to it.

With all clean again and the usual cups of tea to wash down the hastily scoffed hot pie. It was a good thing that we never had much time to eat these meat pies since any delay in the devouring thereof might well have led to inspection of the contents and greatly increasing the chance of a bilious attack. They always went down particularly well after the removal of a badly decomposed body since one's sense of smell was in a state of recession.

Ready, loaded with sparkling cars and drivers enough, we made haste to start the next job. I waited at the front door of the shop, as usual, for the lads to drive round from the garage at the rear of the block. I waited and waited.

Eventually, I walked through to find the cars still in the garage, doors open and a car blocking our exit. They had been looking for the owner for some time now and had drawn a blank. The trolley jack was right at the back of the garage and was only to be used as a last resort but by now, time was getting precious. I had also lost a driver. He had gone looking for the owner of the offending vehicle and had not been seen for some minutes.

The owner of the car arrived and apologised for his thoughtless action and moved his car. We were still short of a driver.

"Shall I go and look for him?" said a helpful voice.

"Over your dead body!" I said, "Take the hearse and first 'Lim' round to the front of the shop and one of you come back for the second car." This would at least get things moving so that when the wayward driver returned, we would be ready for the 'off'.

The minutes were now passing relentlessly and I was breaking into 'emergency time' and we hadn't left the garage. The errant employee returned at the same time as the first man arrived to collect the second car.

"Good!" I said, "Let's get going, see you at the front!" as I made my way through to collect my 'silk' and gloves.

Standing in the front showroom looking at hearse, first and third limousines, I waited. The first limousine driver came through from the garage, having let the other man out, locked the garage doors and took his place in the first car, I waited. I glanced furtively at my wrist to find that Mickey's tennis racquet was nearly at his feet and we were due to arrive at the house over two miles away within the next few moments. Where was the car?

The route between the garage and front doors was via one crossroads junction and a traffic lit "T" junction and I noticed that there was no traffic emanating from the road that led to the garage. Something was afoot. I walked back around the corner to find three men wearing the different but all blue uniforms of London Transport, the post office and a well-known transport company discussing the finer points of driving whilst their vehicles engaged in much more amorous adventures being firmly 'Cheek to Cheek'. The drivers were waiting the arrival of yet another blue uniform.

In the few moments that had elapsed since the fracas, a number of drivers of vehicles behind the trio were offering advice in various languages, volumes and tones. I found my wayward lad firmly stuck in this lot. Mickey's racquet was now firmly back and ready for the overhead smash in twenty minutes, this was the time we were supposed to be in church. There was nothing to do but panic.

In today's world of fast computer controlled everything, instant food, printing, cash, credit and "while you wait dentistry," we never really expect anything to be completed to the first estimated time, the funeral trade is somewhat different.

To explain, if you are plagued by a leaky tap and a call for a plumber and a Monday afternoon and are given an appointment for Tuesday afternoon, you will still be happy to see that tradesman when he eventually makes it to your door on Thursday. However, with the funeral profession, if you are ten minutes late, the phone will be ringing and the attitudes of the callers will range from concern to anger. I wondered what my receptionist would be going through and what excuses would be made.

Eying up the situation, I realised that there was only one way out of this predicament and told my driver to watch for my signal, I also told him that I would meet him at another intersection nearer the start of the funeral when he was free of this 'snarl up'.

Using my local knowledge, I went up to the six or more cars between my car and the nearest intersection and asked them where they were travelling to an offered them an alternative route. For those wanting the Islington direction, it went, "If you turn right here, pass the Downs on your left, under the railway, take a left, carry on two miles until a 'T' junction and turn right, you will avoid this traffic."

I sighed with relief as each car disappeared and my limousine came slowly closer. "I want Stratford!" said the last guy. "If you turn right here, take the first on the left, pass the green on your right, right at the end and left at the lights, you will be back on the same road," I said with final relief.

"You're a bl**&y liar, that will put me straight back onto the end of this lot!" he said with a grin, "But I can see what you're trying to do, anyway, you've done me a favour by getting rid of those others. Good Luck," as he shot off with a smile and a wave.

My man was now free to move, I waved him by as I ran back to the waiting cars at the front of the shop.

The 'Boys in Blue' had arrived at the scene in force, some were sorting out the "shunt" whilst others were trying to get the traffic to move. One "helpful" officer was "assisting" my hearse driver.

"You can't stop 'ere."

"I can't go anywhere without the guvner!"

"Well, you'll have to move!"

"Where?"

"You could go round the corner and wait there."

"If I were to do that, my guvner would get very annoyed with your guvner and we both be in trouble, anyway here he comes, we'll be off in a minute. T'ra."

"Afternoon officer," I said, getting into the hearse, "Drive on, driver," shutting the door.

"—Drive on!"

"There is a policeman standing in front of the hearse," said Ed.

"What a silly place to leave one. Did you leave him there?" I beckoned to the Sargent standing nearby.

"You've left one of your men on the road!" I called. This is where a straight face comes in. "Can you move him? I've got a hot date at the crematorium!" Reality shone a smile through the rule book that had held the tight lips and fixed stare. Off we went.

"How do you get away with it?" asked Ed, the grin on his face stretched all the way to his bald patch.

We were now off and travelling as fast as several litres of internal combustion would carry us. We met the second car at the appointed place and continued on to the house. The relatives had been forewarned of the delay, as had the church and cemetery. There were no delays at the house and very soon, we were off again, the church being the next stop. Half an hour late at the house had changed to twenty minutes at the church so we were doing as well as could be expected.

We took coffin and mourners into the church and settled them down for the service whilst we dashed outside to turn the cars round to be ready for the last part of the journey. This was a fairly narrow street with cars parked on both sides of the road except just outside the church where space had been left for us to park during the service.

The men were all experienced in the art of turning four vehicles around to face the other way and still remain in the same order, with hired limousines this was not too important, however, it does look much better if the hearse is at the front. They had made three attempts at getting to the nearest junction, which was a "T" junction to operate the manoeuvre and on each occasion had been thwarted by an impatient motorist and returned to their parking slot to let them pass. They left the road to clear for a few minutes and the first limousine driver decided that this was a good time to find the toilet.

The road was clear but the driver had not returned from his natural break so I decided that I would take his car and we all made a dash for the junction. The narrowness of the roads meant that we would have to drive the whole cortege past and then reverse it all back around the corner before making our way back to the church. The width of the streets would mean that the whole operation would have to be carried out before any other vehicle came near.

We passed the junction successfully and the rear two cars backed into the side street and were forced to stop when an elderly lady drove up behind them, failing to see what havoc she was causing, our manoeuvre came to a halt. There was nothing for it but to reverse the first two cars back to the church and have another try when the road had cleared again. I reversed the Rolls at high speed since another car was approaching from the direction of the church and should this get to the church before me, it might well be necessary to drive the whole cortege round as very large block indeed.

As I approached the church with two and a half tons of Rolls Royce hurtling backwards, I noticed that the church gates were open and would allow me to complete my turn without going back to the "T" junction. I sped toward the gates, slowly as I approached in order to signal to the approaching car that they would have to wait whilst we cleared the road. The hearse was now not far away so I made my way to the gates and would bump up the kerb as I swung in. I had completed this operation successfully and was feeling pleased with myself when I noticed that the limousine driver was having trouble keeping a straight face.

"What's the matter with you?" I asked in an abrupt tone.

"Nothing," he said innocently. "But I would like to know how you are going to tell the relatives why you ran over their beautiful floral pillow with both tyres!"

An experienced eye could actually tell back two tyres had indeed passed over the wreath. However, this was not my immediate concern. BLOOMIN HECK!

To make matters worse, two mourners chose that precise moment to arrive at the church, albeit late. They looked at the flattened flora with disdain as they handed over their own tribute to be placed with the others, obviously wondering what fate might await their offering.

Using what little time was left of the service, we restructured and repaired and generally did our best to make a wreck look presentable.

Apart from that, the day went well.

A very funny story that was told to me by Frank from when he was working for his previous company. They were dealing with the funeral of an Italian woman. The husband, the only mourner, had very poor command of the English language and the conductor of the funeral had had great trouble in making the arrangements accordingly.

The burial was arranged; the priest had conducted the service in the chapel at the cemetery, rather than having a full service in church with only one attending. The coffin had been lowered into the grave and the final committal said, the husband then looked at the undertaker inquiringly and asked in broken English, "Where is fire?"

The word 'fire' had not entered the arranger's head since the person was assumed to be a Catholic on account of his being Italian and burial had been assumed. The awful realisation that the husband had intended cremation now dawned. The coffin was pulled quickly from the grave and the hearse was called back to return it and the body to the undertaker's premises.

The cemetery authority was very helpful in that they agreed the burial had not actually taken place and therefore Home Office permission for the exhumation would not be necessary. Technically, once the coffin is put in the ground, an exhumation order would be required before it could be taken from the earth.

After the formalities of cremation papers had been completed, the body was cremated and the ashes returned to Italy, which is what the poor, confused husband had intended from the outset.

When dealing with the third or fourth funeral for the same family, one tends to relax a little and sometimes a little too much. I had arranged three funerals for this one family and almost become friends with a couple in their fifties who had lost mother, father and aunt within a very short space of time. All funerals were about the same and the one I was engaged in had been arranged almost completely by telephone.

Hearse and two limousines, cremation and take them all back to their home in Woodford, some miles away. All very simple and the staff are always treated very well and were therefore on their best behaviour.

We collected the flowers and family from the home in Hackney and made our way directly to the crematorium; it was a beautiful sunny day in spring and the flowers were as bright and fresh as they could be.

We drove into the crematorium as usual, I went into the office where I would usually be greeted by a cheery, "Hello, Julian, how are you?"

This day was a little different.

"Hello, Julian, what can we do for you?" This instilled doubt in my mind.

"You aren't expecting me, are you?" I asked Mr Willis.

"No and, in fact, we aren't expecting anyone at all."

"Can I use the phone?" I asked as I made a grab for the instrument. The number took an age to dial and was, of course, engaged. I tried again on another line and was answered promptly.

"Hello, Deb, where am I supposed to be? I'm at Manor Park and they aren't expecting me!" It turned out that I should be at the City of London Crematorium. OOPS!

I made my thanks, walked out of the office and up to the hearse in the normal manner. As I stepped into the hearse, I said to the driver, "Try and look cool, hang a 'U' turn and take me to the City of London!"

"Oh dear, did we make a mistake?" said the driver with more than the usual tone of sarcasm in his voice.

"Less of the 'we'," I corrected, "You're supposed to be driving, so you should know where we are going."

"Silly me," he replied. "It must be my fault this close to payday!"

We both had a little chuckle to ourselves, made our way to the other crematorium, apologised to the relatives and gave ourselves no points out of ten for route planning.

As usual, news of our error trickled its way around the trade at the speed of light. However, I consoled myself with the knowledge that I was not the only person to have done such a thing. One undertaker, who shall be nameless, was purported to have gone to three wrong cemeteries at the same funeral.

Chapter Ten
People, Places and Buildings

All this frivolity about funerals, staff and the goings on behind the scenes is often overshadowed by the things people say whilst making arrangements or at the funeral, being in a state of shock can often give rise to words emanating from relatives mouths without the slightest thought being given to the content. There is also no thought given to the poor undertaker's composure, after, all he is only doing his job when people keep trying their best to make him collapse in fits of the giggles.

One Saturday, as I was looking forward to a quiet pint or seven in the 'local', a man with a strong accent from an island just west of Wales stepped in to make arrangements for the funeral of his late wife.

"I want to see the undertaker," he said in demanding terms. Now, this man had just walked into a building situated between a pub and a car spares shop, the window of which was adorned with memorial stones and pictures of horse driven hearses, over the door of this shop, the words 'Funeral Directors' and 'Monumental Masons' were prominently displayed.

Although I was wearing a grey suit, I was also wearing a black tie and white shirt and obviously waiting to equip all who came through my door with vast quantities of fish and chips.

"Yes, sir, please come in and take a seat." I ushered him into the main office and drew up a chair in front of my desk. I sat down in my own chair and withdrew a form from one of the drawers on which to take details of the funeral arrangements.

"Can I take your full name sir?"

"I don't know what you want my name for, it's my wife what's died!" he said loudly.

I asked again, saying that I would need his name for the records and that I would also like to call him by his name rather than a formal "sir" during the interview.

"Murphy, John Murphy," came the reply.

"And what was your wife's name, Mr Murphy?" came my next question in the order of things that I needed to know.

There was a lengthy pause in which the man looked around the seemingly bored with the whole situation. His attitude also reflected the impression that he was dealing with the 'lad' rather than the boss. At last his eyes focused firmly on me, he drew breath and prepared himself for the answer, "—Mrs Murphy!" his brogue was stronger and face had an irritated look.

For my part, I had to avert my gaze and pull my cheeks in firmly to avoid releasing the eruptions of laughter gathering in me.

It was not the general public who had a monopoly on the ridiculous, one of the most obviously silly statements came from a member of the cloth. The term used in the trade to describe such a man ministering funeral rites is, in fact, 'The Sky Pilot' but don't tell Rev. David Rhodes because he doesn't think it's very funny.

One reverend and elderly gentleman worked for the local hospital and as such would get to know the patients and their relatives during the very difficult times when death was imminent. Because of this close contact with the family, they would often ask if he could minister the funeral rites for them; usually, he would agree.

Since he was such a busy person at the hospital, we would normally arrange to collect him from the hospital at an appointed time as we passed on our way to the cemetery and the hearse would drop him back there immediately after the service. We were never let down by these arrangements but I often wondered what people passing by must have thought when a funeral cortege came to a halt in the narrow main road in front of the general hospital and see a fully robed priest running across the road from the hospital to take his place in one of the passing limousines.

During the few moments when he and I were alone, we would always enquire about each other's well-being and often pass comment on the weather or appreciate the colours of spring or autumn around us. One day as we were walking together from the graveside to the car, he took my arm firmly and said in a very "matter of fact" tone of voice, "Do you know, that hospital is full of very sick people?"

"I hope that doesn't include the staff," I said, with more than a little frivolity in my voice.

"Oh," he replied calmly, "I suppose that was a bit of a silly thing to say, wasn't it?" We walked on.

One of the few pleasures left in the lonely life of an undertaker is to cause havoc on the roads, either by travelling very slowly and holding up a long line of traffic at a snail's pace or by bringing it to a complete halt, preferably during the rush hour.

Early one sunny morning, we had the good fortune to start the funeral of a West Indian on a main road in Leyton, a suburb of East London. This road was one of the major routes across the area toward the centre of the capital, the road was quite narrow for the traffic that it was expected to take, there were plenty of parked cars on either side to make matters better and we had an ample supply of limousines.

We arrived at the street a few blocks away from the house, it was already full of slow-moving traffic, city bound. After a few moments, a car stopped and waved us to go in front of him. Hearse and all five limousines strode cheerfully into the throng of the traffic.

"He's going to regret that very, very soon!" I said to the hearse driver.

"How long have you allowed at the house to load up?" inquired Ed.

"About half an hour."

"Then I think that there is going to be an awful lot of lateness for work today!"

"Can't be helped, this is a Mosses funeral."

We stopped outside the house where the floral tributes stretched into the neighbours' gardens on both sides, people were still arriving in their droves with armfuls of flowers, albeit now, from only one direction. I managed to find the chief mourners and we started to load the flowers onto the hearse and cars, it looked at one time as if we were not gaining on the arriving tributes but we could always ask for help from the private car drivers.

It took nearly all the allotted thirty minutes to load up with flowers and mourners, during which time, the odd car managed to squeeze past in the opposite direction, thus keeping the greater and more urgent flow of city bound traffic at bay behind the cortege.

We were ready to go and I was standing in front of the hearse, ready to page the cortege from the house, when a young man driving a car in the opposite direction spoke to me.

"'Ere, you're famous. They've just mentioned you on the 'Flying Eye'. You're holding up traffic right back to the North Circular Road and to the M 11!" A distance of about two miles.

The Flying Eye is the traffic spotter aeroplane that works for a London radio station. I was most impressed and we had a good laugh about it all the way to the church. The remainder of the day was boring by comparison.

Now some of us like a good sing. Any number of people will sing along to some boring popular song or melody. However, Graham and I were a little more selective about what we sang along to. Our Graham, although not a churchgoer, except when being paid for it, believed in the life hereafter whilst I am quite convinced that it all ends with decomposition, after all, spirits come in bottles, don't they?

Our favourites with which to join in a rousing chorus, were 'Jerusalem', 'Onward Christian Soldiers' and 'For those in Peril on the sea'. Unfortunately, the latter did not come up very often as they are not exactly 'intrepid' on the river Lea in Hackney.

Waiting in the church porches for the service to run their course was where we had our greatest choristry, however, standing, shivering in wet, windy and cold church porches did often make the line "In England's green and pleasant land" a little difficult to sing with any gusto. We always assumed when, at full voice, the mourners within the church would also be in good voice and that any assistance from without would not be noticed as we always kept to the clean versions so that the words would match.

We never had any complaints from the mourners but, there was one member of my staff who thought it irreverent that we should join in with such obvious enthusiasm and enjoyment. This man was not a member of staff for long, after all, most of us were funeral employees because we had only read as far as the first three letters of the job title.

We could not always enjoy a good sing at a church, however, there were sometimes other entertainments. In our area, there was a sizeable Greek community and local Greek church. With luck, I had managed to build up a good relationship with the local community and I also got on well with the local priest.

Greek people have their own traditions of burial and these stretch from the dressing of the body in a calico smock to the partaking of food and drink before leaving the graveside after the committal. Another tradition is the practice of lighting a candle in church as with most Catholic faiths.

Greek churches are beautifully ornate with their tapestries and scrolls, the regalia is usually finely carved out of wood and gilded, making the interior a very colourful spectacle.

On entering the church, all mourners file past the candle box, make their offering, collected a candle, light and place it in the sandbox at the back of the church. Our local church had two of these sand boxes and usually, the congregation would be thoughtful about evenly distributing their votive candles between the two boxes. With the involvement in this additional task on entering the church, a queue would form at the door whilst we were well on our way to the trestles and this would often cause our exit from the church and back to the vehicles to be held up by the incoming crowd.

Toward the end of the service, one of the church servers would come to the back and extinguish the candles.

One day, when we had a great number of mourners, it looked for a while as if there would not be enough candles to go around and these little lights were being squeezed into the sandboxes, closer and closer together.

At school, we learnt all about conduction, convection and radiation and taking two out of three of these confusing terms and applying them to a candle merely states that hot things will heat things around them and that hot air rises, the latter being the only reason the roof of the Houses of Parliament stays up.

As hot air rises around a candle and the candle next to it, the flames will tend to lean toward each other since there is not enough air between the two to sustain the updraught requirements of both candles. If there are a substantial number of candles in close proximity to each other, they will all work together in creating this updraught and thus act like a bellows does to a blacksmith's forge.

On this one occasion, the candles were so close together and the updraught became so fierce, the flames that were already burning with a ferocity that was making the wax boil, almost became one huge column of fire reaching upward within the church and creating a furnace like roar. Maintaining my composure and calm, my immediate reaction was to run. However, the church server approached looking calmer than the corpse and proceeded to pick up handfuls of these firebrands and quench their heads in the sand. The conflagration ceased.

At the end of the Greek service, the entire congregation would file past the coffin and kiss both the sacred church bible and a crucifix placed on the head of the coffin before returning to their seats and waiting to follow the procession out of the church.

Outside, there was always a great deal of weeping and wailing whilst we tried to get the mourners sat in their places for the onward journey. Sometimes, a major deity would assist with a liberal sprinkling of cold rainwater. The cemetery usually chosen was a fair distance from Hackney, since there was a special section for Greek people within the cemetery itself.

At the graveside, the length of the committal was fairly short, however, as with most burials, the time taken over this part was always directly proportional to the temperature of that day or inversely proportional to the rate of rainfall.

Immediately after this was over, everyone would return to the cars and people would appear with wine, sherry, cheese, bread and olives. These delicacies would be passed around the assembled multitude, including the undertaker's staff and the gravediggers. We would all pay our respects to the dead and drink to the health of the living in his fashion before returning home. What a civilised practice.

At the beginning of my sentence on the realms of Human Disposal, whilst Bob was still manager, the Hackney area was in a much worse state of dilapidation than it is now. There were many houses where people had lived all their lives and even some whose parents had lived in that same house for most of their lives too.

Very often, these houses would be inhabited by sisters, now elderly, who, for one reason or another had never married and moved away or alternatively, their husband's had been killed in one of the very popular wars of the first half of the century and they had ended up back at the ancestral home.

Invariably, these houses were steeped in history and should anyone lift any of the ancient, worn out but spotlessly clean oil cloth (the trade name linoleum came later than this stuff), they would most probably be able to supply the local museum with neatly pressed copies of newspapers and magazines covering any topic from the Churchill to Chamberlain, (not Winston, Randolph).

Three such sisters lived in a house in Clapton Square where the remaining few houses in the terrace were under renovation, the balconies of the houses under repair were removed, the brickwork was cleaned and repointed, roofs repaired, windows renewed and still, the sister's house on the end of the block had no electricity and, I believe, no gas either. It was all overgrown with ivy on the outside and, although rather dingy on the inside with its dark floor and wall coverings, nevertheless clean.

When one of these sisters died at home, we moved her back to our chapel and the funeral was arranged. On the appointed time and day of the funeral, we arrived at the house at the same time as an ambulance. This vehicle looked rather out of place, but was there to take another of the sisters to the hospital after she had collapsed. We continued the funeral with only the one sister in attendance. The other, happily recovered to live on for a few more years.

When eventually, all three sisters had passed on, the house was beautifully renovated and remains to this day, the only one on that terrace with a cast iron balcony.

Another similar house was on Newick Road, just opposite my shop. Only once did I have the pleasure to enter this magnificent dwelling. This was a real portal to the past. The lady who had been resident had died in hospital and the arrangements had been made by one of the nieces, an elegant and charming middle-aged woman.

It was always pleasantly refreshing to deal with people who maintained their composure during these difficult times because they appreciated genuine sympathy at their personal loss whilst agreeing with the selfishness of keeping their loved one from their Valhalla. I, therefore, was feeling very proud to be involved with the funeral arrangements and, having made certain that everything was "just so," we set off for the house.

I was met at the door by the woman and her husband who pointed out the very few flowers that were to be taken with us. "Mother hated cut flowers, but we thought the coffin would look rather bare without anything."

They had bought a beautiful four foot cross and some of the relatives had brought simple sprays and arrangements. Otherwise, the request had been "Family flowers only and donations to—"

I have always wondered why there is a feeling that attendance at a funeral is accompanied by the requirement to spend money, granted that flowers are a tradition and brighten up the occasion, however, if no flowers are requested, then why should this be assumed to be replaced by anything other than a card of sympathy.

I now started to look around the house, we had a little time since we were still waiting for some people to arrive from "over the water." In London, people who live on either side of the Thames think that people who live on the other side are slightly odd and can never understand how "they" can never understand the road patterns, whilst their own side of the river remains perfectly logical.

The house that I was standing in, was virtually a museum dating back to the early 1900s. The front door was a work of art with its multicoloured leaded panels in excellent condition. The hallway had a small neat dresser with a hat stand and umbrella rack, large pictures hung on the wall in magnificent frames. I was ushered through to the living room somehow, because the size of the furniture was smaller than that of today, the rooms looked larger than did similar rooms in other houses in the street that were filled with modern settees and armchairs.

The dining room had a large dining table in the centre surrounded with high-backed chairs in excellent condition, the table had a heavy cover over it, the walls were papered in a charcoal grey with greyish white motifs and hung with large paintings similar to those in the hall, there were glass fronted rosewood cabinets bearing interesting silver items, heavy drapes hung beside the bay window whilst net curtains covered the panes whilst allowing plenty of natural light to diffuse into the room. I stood in awe.

"Magnificent, isn't it?" said the niece. I closed my mouth for fear of any passing bat looking for a place to spend the night. I regained my composure and moved toward the covered table and reached out with my gloved hand and turning to the niece:

"May I?"

"Please do!" she replied.

I lifted a corner of the drape and beheld a magnificent mahogany table with a tiny inlaid brass line, the polish was perfect and there was not a blemish on any of the surface that I could see.

"I don't suppose it has seen the light of day for more than a few hours since it first got here," she said.

We moved into the parlour where the scene was of a similar vintage, the small window in the corner extended into a tiny gazebo overlooking the garden. The wallpaper and pictures were very much the same as elsewhere in the house, small tables stood beside the parlour chairs and the inevitable piano stood behind the door. The fireplaces in both rooms were marble and ornate, nothing had been done to destroy their beauty as with many other houses in the area. Each fireplace had its original overthrow and the tiny shelves were adorned with little ornaments. I stood there awaiting another bat.

This was the most beautifully unspoilt house I ever had the pleasure to enter, it really should have been opened as a museum by the borough, however, it was probably stripped of its treasures sold and probably modernised in accordance with the requirements of life today.

It seems that it was always on a Saturday morning that the most memorable people chose to make arrangements for their loved ones, either they are being considerate of their relatives not losing too much time at work or maybe they are just tidy people and think it right that they should finish the week before they 'pop off'.

It was one such Saturday morning that a man and woman came into the office. The woman I had met many years before but, unusually, could not place her in my memory. The man, a jolly 'bear' of a man with a large bushy beard, both were very well dressed and well spoken. Their mother had died on the previous day and they had been and "done the rounds" of hospital and registrar and, happily for me, arrived well in time for me to take details before sneaking off for the odd jarful of brown fluid. What a thoroughly considerate family!

We discussed at length the local cemeteries and what they had to offer, both Brother and Sister agreed that they did not like any of the East London cemeteries, they did not like the idea of cemeteries within London and asked about "out of town" cemeteries.

This is where problems can arise. Private cemeteries tend to be within the London area and the outlying areas are often served by municipal cemeteries who hold the land for burial, either exclusively for their parishioners or will only sell to outsiders at very high prices. There is one such authority that will treble prices to non-parishioners, making the idea impossible to nearly all.

This family was adamant that their mother was going to be buried in a small cemetery, whatever the cost. Somehow and by sheer luck, I had been dealing with the Epping Forest District Council for the reopening of a grave for an additional interment some months earlier and, during the conversation with the jolly and helpful lady at the council office, she had offered to send details of grave prices to me. Whilst casting an eye over this document, I noticed how cheap the graves were in comparison to London cemeteries, even when the price was adjusted for non-parishioners.

At the mention of Chigwell, the relative's eyes lit up and they eagerly accepted my suggestion. We were able to choose the coffin and the number of cars. However, the choice of grave and church were left for me to arrange the following week when the council offices opened. They would take a trip out to the cemetery over the weekend and have a look. It had been a good day, a few moments after they left, I was testing the ale in the local hostelry as part of my service to the community. It has probably been noticed by now that there has been mention of many trips to the "local" but not many FROM. Customary replies as a riposte to silly comments may be found in previous chapters.

I received a telephone call on the Sunday from the family, eagerly expressing approval of the proposed cemetery, they had also chosen the church and provided me with the telephone number of the vicar to whom they had already spoken and arranged the date. I pointed out that this was a little premature since I had not yet spoken to the cemetery authority and we could end up looking very silly having to wait outside the cemetery gates for a day or two between service and burial if the authority could not fit us or more accurately, the coffin, in!

On the Monday, I was able to arrange the time proposed by family and vicar with the cemetery authority and left messages with both parties to confirm the same. The date was for the following Friday. We arranged the coffin and linings, collected "mum" and presented her in the chapel, ready for the few who might come in. We had been told that both son and daughter had seen Mum at the hospital and did not wish to see her again. I felt that there would be some traffic to our chapel.

Later that evening, the vicar called to say that he had arranged Thursday with the family and not Friday, he could not change to the Friday, even if they wanted to as he already had a previous engagement. So much for mice, men and plans. I now had a dilemma, try to change the cemetery date to please the vicar or the church to please the cemetery and most likely, end up upsetting two out of three. I had to wait to contact the family that evening. The first person I managed to contact was the sister that I had not met, so I asked her for advice.

Over the next twenty-four hours, many phone calls were bandied back and forth until we settled on moving the day up one to the Thursday and everyone was as happy as could be expected.

All went smoothly and on the day of the funeral, we arrived at the house and I immediately remembered where I had met the daughter before; it had been at her husband's funeral some five years before. The 'jolly bear' was in the park, opposite the house, where he, as a keen photographer and journalist, was busy taking records of the front covers of the daily papers against the background of the local park in summer together with snaps of our arrival and the loading of the flowers.

With the journalistic influence in command, it was not surprising to find that a considerable amount of refreshments were available for consumption by relatives, friends and any unsuspecting undertaker that might pass by. In view of the distance we had to travel and the number of people involved in the funeral itself, we declined the offer of things alcoholic prior to the service.

The funeral all went well with the exception of the first limousine driver, who, on leaving the church en route to the cemetery via a very steep driveway from the churches back gate, had engaged the handbrake with such gusto that he was unable to release the same when the time came to move on. The hearse had moved out into the road, alone and with the only sign of a cortege, being the nose of a reluctant limousine peering up the slope and across the road.

The gate of the church was only just sufficiently wide to allow the limousine to pass through with minimal clearance on either side so that I was unable to jump in and assist, the handbrake being to the left of the driver's seated position. I glanced at the mourners in the back to see the men seated in the front row beaming smiles of great amusement at our predicament.

Following the statutory five second panic, the only way I could see out of this position was to back up all the cars behind and allow the car to be run back down to the level ground.

Having cleared the space behind, I went back to Ed in the limousine and told him to take the car out of gear, move to the passenger seat whilst keeping his right foot firmly on the footbrake. From this better vantage point, he was able to use two hands on the handbrake, release it and let the car run slowly back into the space behind before taking a second run at the exit whilst I made sure that the road was clear for our escape. It all looked very ungainly and amateurish to me but seemed to furnish the mourners with untold joy.

Our arrival at the cemetery was an anti-climax by comparison and all went very smoothly. They were all very pleased with the cemetery and requested my assurance that the grave was for two people. The son said jokingly that there would now be a "race" for the other space between the other members of the family.

The journey back to Hackney was uneventful but the funeral breakfast was memorable. This family's way of dealing with the passing of a loved one was to have a party with good food, live music and much laughter. Photographs were passed around, childhood stories told and mother's passing was celebrated in a uniquely joyful manner.

A few weeks later, I was pleased to greet the daughter when she arrived at my office, I assumed that she had arrived to settle the funeral account. I, therefore, greeted her with a smile. We sat down and I had already found the account when she told me that she had not come to pay the bill but to arrange another funeral, this time for her bother, the 'jolly bear' who had died of a heart attack the previous day. She said that she had felt a wince when they had jokingly said about the 'race' for the other space in the grave.

Be careful what you wish for!

_____-

Chapter Eleven
Another Fine Mess!

Hopefully, most funeral goers and that will eventually be most of us, the term, of course, referring to the willing rather that unwitting participant for we all have to go that way sometime, will experience a smooth, well-prepared event when the presence of the undertaker and his staff will go virtually unnoticed.

Others have experienced disasters of varying magnitude, some are easily sorted out, others are not. Some are avoidable, some inevitable through carelessness or misunderstanding. Some require an apology, others will require more tactful handling and there are those which will invoke weird and wonderful incantations from the funeral director which as a rough translation will normally go as follows:

"Dear God, please let the ground open and swallow me up a long with the other idiots who are responsible for this bloody mess!"

This can be said to be similar in many walks of life and many other businesses, however, when some daft bearer has just slipped on something he should have been looking for, dropped the box, the top of which has come off turfing any part or all of Granny out into a muddy puddle, trying to act nonchalant, whistle casually and saying "Sorry, we don't usually do it this way" doesn't cut it with any of the relatives or friends.

Promising to get another box and try again is better but not fully acceptable and casually rolling the corpse into the grave along with the broken remains of the box whilst assuring the relative that nobody will be able to tell the difference when the grave is filled is completely out!

Similarly, asking the relatives for fifty pence for the gas and a match is not advisable at a crematorium in an effort to cheer up distress. As a method of displaying your regret, Hari Kiri is also unacceptable, as is flaying your staff alive on the spot.

Coffins and caskets are made in various sizes to fit the needs of the individuals, so if a person you have just met informs you that his occupation is a 'timber tailor', think carefully before asking silly questions. Cemetery authorities usually ask to be supplied with the outside dimensions of the box so that the grave can be dug to fit fairly neatly, they are also fairly good at cutting the shape well enough to make the whole thing look a snug fit when the coffin is lowered into place.

The neatest grave I ever saw was in Plumstead Cemetery in clay where the sides were cut showing neat and even spade marks all the way round and I have even seen graves lined with grass all the way down, giving a really lovely effect. Sometimes things go wrong!

Since a coffin has the foot flared out at an angle, the largest piece of the box is the lid, so, if the hole is slightly too small and the coffin is lowered in awkwardly, the lid, held in place with four small screws, is normally the first thing to catch.

At this point, it is the job of the bearer feeling his lowering web becoming light, to quietly call a halt, lift gently and try to lower again. Failure to do this can result in the coffin becoming wedged in the hole at a very odd angle. The heavier the coffin, the worse it can be and if care is not taken promptly, even the smoothest running funeral can now go drastically wrong. The lid can now be in great danger of coming off and allowing the rest of the box to continue downward.

Placing a large boot on the lid and giving it a firm shove is inadvisable unless you can rely on all the assembled mourners to remain looking the other way and asking the gravedigger to jump on it is completely out of the question!

The only satisfactory solution is to remove the coffin from the grave, suffer the immediate embarrassment, find the digger and calmly request the grave be recut to allow free passage of the dear departed downward.

There is another consideration for the funeral director to take into account at this point, the minister. Experienced funeral ministers can go through the service without a glance at a text and may well be gazing upward at the time of a hiccup. Less experienced ministers, however, could equally be completely engrossed in the prayer book to notice.

In the full flood of, "For as much, therefore, as it hath ('has' for the younger clergy) pleased Almighty God in his great mercy, to take from us the soul of our dear brother/sister—we therefore commit his/her body to the ground. Earth to earth, ashes to ashes, dust to dust." ("If the Lord don't get you the Devil must" is usually on the lips of the funeral staff at this point.)

The minister then looking around to find, not only is the coffin now out of the grave and back in full daylight, but also, there is a perfectly fit human being in the grave armed with shovel and muttering, "I'm not ready for the Almighty yet, you idiot!"

There are other exciting things that can happen at the point of committal, these have included: the staging around the grave giving way when any number of bearers and/or clergy will forget the job in hand instantly to concentrate on self-preservation with varying amusing results.

An aircraft can pass overhead noisily, leaving the mourners looking at each other and wondering whether their dear one has been buried or not or the webbing can be too short for the depth of the grave when the front row mourners will have been much more interested in why one of the bearers has suddenly decided to take to his knees firmly clutching the end of the web and reaching into the grave to have taken any interest in what was being said by the minister at all.

In the crematorium, where the catafalque is high, it is customary to carry the coffin in and on reaching the end of their carry, the bearers at the foot will bend forward from the waist, placing the foot of the coffin on the first roller, sometimes they will bend a little too low when the soft music and dulcet tones of the minister's "I am the resurrection and the life saith ('said' for the younger clergy) the Lord" will be rudely interrupted by a loud THUD usually accompanied by a groan from at least one of the bearers.

Alternatively, some 'foot' men can have a habit of lifting an arm around the coffin at this point, this has resulted in the hand becoming trapped between coffin and catafalque and a loud 'AARGH' being added to the service.

Church trestles can be fun too, the aisles are narrow in small churches and the trestles can be old and rickety. Bearers arriving at this point are always on full view, as they are either in the church already or following closely behind the coffin. It is the job of the funeral director to usher the mourners to their places as the coffin is being placed on the rests as the minister is well into "He that believeth ('believes' for the younger clergy) in Me shall never die—" being accompanied by the clattering sound of trestles resounding in the nave and bearers muttering, "Back a bit, no, to me, hold it" and "Hold it there while I pick it up!"

Coats get caught up and fingers too, novice bearers get pushed into odd corners, shoulder pads spend entire services dangling out obtrusively from under the coffin like a macabre flag of death. During the service music can start and stop at odd intervals when the switching off the speaker system, people can arrive in the vestibule and loudly enquire about the time of somebody's funeral in a very quiet point in the service with attendants putting their bit in with an even louder "SHHHH!"

Worst of all and this is surprisingly common, a rift in the family at some time has resulted in one of the relatives not being informed that the funeral is taking place, often they arrive with fire and venom, burst into the service and start a fight on the spot. Most entertaining, but what can you do about it, a brawl starts in the chapel and all you can do is keep out of it whilst trying to keep a straight face with cheeks firmly clenched between teeth.

There are very few occasions when the coffin does not fit the body, but it does happen. We had to do the funeral of a person who had died in circumstances when the body had become badly decomposed, the relatives had been told that there would be no chance to view but had chosen an expensive coffin, this had been ordered and prepared whilst the body had been sent to the public mortuary for storage prior to the funeral about a week later.

The lads went to the mortuary a few hours before the funeral, on their return, their faces were not happy ones. The refrigeration units at the public mortuary had gone wrong and frozen everything solid. Our customer had been left on his side with a bend in his back. He was not going to help at all. We went out on the morning of the funeral in the hopes that the warm weather would help our predicament. On our return, it had not!

Remembering my secondary school physics and that pressure creates heat, we applied as much pressure as we could to the arms and legs to try and make the limbs bend to facilitate the required fit as we only needed a couple of inches to get the body in the coffin and the lid on. Had we been dogs, we would have been making a great deal of noise in the entirely wrong arboretum, to expand a well-known phrase or saying!

"Well, it's only a couple of inches, can't we stretch the sides of the box and try to get the lid on?" enquired a helpful soul.

It was worth a try, anything was, as time was running out and I was at a complete loss as to how I might try to explain my way out of this to the waiting relatives. With one of us on each side of the box and the erstwhile occupant, half in and half out at an odd angle, we pulled.

Very soon, we had some good news and some bad news. Taking the good news first, the body had slipped to below the lid level of the coffin and was wedged there. The bad news was that the coffin itself had joined in with a loud CRACK!

"So far, so what," someone said, breaking the long silence.

We tried the lid. It fitted well enough end to end but was a little short on the sides. A glance at the wrist assured me that time had not come to a halt and a close examination showed that we were not all that far out. All we needed to do was to remove the moulding around the lid and make it cover the bare wood visible at the top edge of the sides of the coffin.

Had this been a cremation, we could have tacked the moulding back around the side of the coffin since at no time do people ever see the top of the coffin and copious quantities of flowers could hide a multitude of sins. It was, of course, a burial. We heaved the moulding around to cover as much of the offending unpolished wood as we could. It didn't look too bad and a blind man wearing dark glasses at night would never have noticed a thing.

Having done our best, we ventured out on the job with all the staff primed to make sure that any floral tribute that could be put on the coffin would be and at all times, at least one bearer would be between relatives and the coffin. If anyone noticed, they did not say, but there were one or two times when I did wonder.

Even when you have taken what would seem all precautions to ensure that things go smoothly, someone somewhere who wants a letter from you, urgently, will not get it, even with the 'Special Delivery' service that the boys in blue in red vehicles at the Royal Mail are so proud of.

As previously mentioned, Cremation forms have to be deposited with the cremating authority, either the day before the cremation or at latest, arrive by first post on the day of the service. At Christmas, Easter and close to that day in the middle of February when the Royal Mail earn most of their reliably large profits or during times of bad weather and postal disputes, we would always throw caution into some vehicle or another and hand deliver these forms ourselves but reliance on the special service would usually come good at other times.

On the day before cremations were to take place, if the crematorium had not received the forms by second post, they would always telephone and enquire about their whereabouts. It was usually a matter of saying that they had been posted the day before and should be expected the following morning or that they went out that day by the prized 'Special Delivery'.

One day we had the call in the afternoon when the papers had been sent by the magic service on the previous day and I had expected that they had already been processed. It was getting late in the day and I grabbed the telephone to try and locate the envelope, the counterfoil had a number on it, name and address of both sender and addressee, together with a lot of small print.

Whilst trying to contact someone in charge of the postal service, which I can only describe as being akin to looking for a policeperson when you want one, I started to read the fine details. They do not guarantee to deliver the next day but do promise to refund the cost of the special service if they fail and you can be bothered to fill in giving more details than might be expected in a divorce contract for Elizabeth Taylor.

I was passed from one person to another, telling my story in full as I went. From what I could gather, they leave a great deal to chance since they could not actually locate the letter by reference to the number and incessantly blamed the computer that I would have thought would have been there to do that precise task.

"We have a record of it leaving Hackney, but no record of it arriving at the local sorting office in the delivery area," some bright spark told me.

"Well, where is it?" I asked and thought immediately that I might be asking an amoeba to explain the 'Theory of Relativity' in braille.

"It's in transit!" came the blatantly obvious retort.

"When is it going to get there?" It was rather like asking the Minister of Defence what were the precise movements of the country's nuclear weapons at that moment, he didn't know, couldn't find out and wouldn't tell you even if he could.

"Will it get there by the morning?" I was getting to precisely where I was already and taking an eternity to do it.

"It may well do."

"Are you thinking of running for any political office?" I gave way to sarcasm as usual. "You should go far." There was a silence at the other end.

"If you find it, would you call me immediately, I am available on this number at all times." He agreed to do this small thing.

The sun came back into visibility via the long way round and the telephone remained stubbornly silent.

We are fully aware that the postal service is working all night but anyone in the vicinity of a customer service telecommunication device goes deaf until about 8 o'clock in the morning. To my great surprise, they hadn't found it.

The funeral was early and so a call to the crematorium and a conversation with the superintendent ended in an agreement that we could continue with the service. However, we would have to take the coffin back afterwards.

The dilemma here was whether to tell the relatives or not. On the one hand, we could assume that the cremation papers would arrive in due course and that nobody would see us taking the coffin out and loading it into the lower deck of the hearse, out of view from the public gaze for the return journey, followed by a candid return when the paperwork had been dealt with.

On the other hand, the form could end up in that elusive post office in the sky, never to be seen again. This would entail the completion of a duplicate set of forms which would have to be signed by the relatives and since the immediate relative was neither blind nor stupid, I didn't rate my chances on being able to get away with going to see them, putting a blindfold on them and asking them to "Sign here" for the records. I erred on the side of caution and told the eldest son the whole story to lay my path clear, should the worst result in what I have come to accept as normal.

On my return to the office after that funeral, my receptionist informed that the crematorium had just called to say that the papers had arrived and we could take the coffin back as soon as we were ready.

Fate is annoyingly reliable!

By now, you will have probably realised that death occurs at almost any time of life, usually towards the end, but no one ever tells you how far you have got at any one time. If you knew, at any time that you were about ninety-seven and a half per cent through, you could make arrangements, you could be in the right place and save everyone a great deal of trouble, you could phone aged aunties that you had always meant to get in touch with and say your goodbyes and forget to pay the credit card bill for a few months, not to mention popping down to the insurance company with a few extra shillings.

Finally, you could slip into the undertakers, make the arrangements for yourself and then leave your body in the right place at the right time. A doctor could be on hand to save any further problems of the coroner being called.

Everyone dies, even those whose relatives are 'Entertaining Her Majesty' as the term goes. This is an expression used to describe that time in some people's lives when they have been fairly naughty and someone has found out. The process then goes through a time when people in wigs and gowns do a lot of talking and decide amongst themselves, how long it is going to be before you can make your own choice of whether to spend a nice quiet evening in the local boozer with friends of your choosing. These people are otherwise known as 'prisoners'.

Dependent on the degree of naughtiness and therefore the place of incarceration, there is, naturally, a varying presence of PLOD. The 'Old Bill' do take great care to be as unobtrusive as possible and a minor offender will be allowed to move fairly freely amongst friends and relatives whilst the attending officers, always in civilian clothes, take a role as onlookers, others are permanently manacled to their guard.

In an effort to conceal the unsightly bi-wristed bracelet, it is normal to throw a coat over the handcuffs as it is still unseemly to expect two grown up and probably large men to hold hands during the entire proceedings.

Children, being so wonderfully naïve, have a different perspective on life and tend to see only the good things. One small child, on seeing two large men carrying one small raincoat, asked his mother, "Mummy, is that a very heavy raincoat?"

"No, dear," hastened the mother in reply.

Undaunted, the child continued the interrogation.

"Then why is it taking two men to carry it?"

A scruffy, balding man came into the office one afternoon, somewhat the worse for drink. The parts of the two different suits he was wearing came from two different eras, not to mention tailors, the outfit had also been cleaner at some time.

It took me some time to confirm that he had actually come to make funeral arrangements, as he was adamant that he only wanted to ask the price.

A substantial amount of the work that we carried out was paid for by the social services and I knew that they would not entertain an estimate that was not fully completed, with the exception if the time and date that the funeral was to take place. Once authorised, it was a simple matter to fill in the gaps.

I finally managed to seat the man in the office. Through the alcoholic haze, I managed to ascertain that the woman who had died was the wife of an old friend who was disabled and therefore could not attend our shop. The old fellah became quite confused with the various addresses involved so there were many false starts and much paper wasted but in the end, I was sure that I had the required details in the correct order, I think!

"Now, sir, take that estimate to your friend's social services department and they will authorise the funeral to go ahead, then you come to see me again and we will arrange some times," I said as he was leaving with our estimate in a clean white envelope that was being stuffed awkwardly into a grubby pocket.

"I take this to Sylvester Road and they let me know?" he said, unsurely. Taking the now crumpled envelope from his pocket and waving it at me.

"No sir, you take that to Mr Thorns's Social Security office in Bethnal Green and they will inform him within the next few days, NOT your local office, they have nothing to do with it, you are dealing with the matter for Mr Thorn."

"Where's Bethnal Green office then?"

"Come back into the office and I will find out." We sat down again whilst I made a few enquiries and supplied the address.

"Where's that?"

The address made enough sense to me that I was able to explain exactly where the office would be in relation to local landmarks.

"Oh, that's where I go for Charlie," came the exasperating reply.

A few days later, I spotted the same suit lurching shabbily towards my office.

"Ah, Mr Box!" I said as I opened the door for him. Much more alcohol had passed his lips this time and I was sure that I was in for a hard time.

The interview this time should have been fairly short, but seemed to take an eternity. Eventually, he left.

"See you on Tuesday, Mr Box," I said as he left.

The office smelt more like a barroom after a heavy evening session.

On the day of the funeral, we arrived at the address to start the funeral to find a derelict and boarded-up house. I tried the door anyway, but in vain. We searched the street for any sign of a flower or somebody who might be anxiously awaiting our arrival. We then made our way to the address Mr Box had given as his own home. Still no joy. Neither person had a telephone.

Eventually, we gave up and went back to the shop, body and all. I telephoned the cemetery, told them of our problem and postponed the funeral until further notice.

The next morning, Mr Box arrived at the office.

"Where were you yesterday?" he asked accusingly and still smelling strongly of alcohol, even at this early hour.

"Well, I was about to ask you the same question," I replied.

"We were in the flat, waiting for you all afternoon."

"No. 2 was a boarded-up house, not a flat," I said in defence.

He gave me a scruffy piece of paper with an address on it. No. 2, Studland Court.

"This is Studland Court, not Romilly Road, the address you gave me was Romilly Road," I said, pointing to the estimate. "Never mind. All we have to do is to make the arrangements for another day."

"How much more is that going to cost?" asked Mr Box. "We can't afford to pay twice."

I was quite touched that he was "in tune" enough to realise that we had already been out to do the funeral.

"Nothing, there was just a misunderstanding and I remember where Studland Court is, but when I tried that door, there was no reply and the music was rather loud so I thought it was the wrong house. Are you sure that you were there?"

"We were there, but maybe we didn't hear you, the old boy is rather deaf."

We arranged the funeral for the following day and this time, all went without a hitch.

Chapter Twelve
Don't Call the Pickfords!

About ninety-two per cent of people die in hospital so the collection of the body is a fairly simple procedure since the hospital porters collect the dead from the bed and remove them to the hospital mortuary. The paperwork is then dealt within the hospital administrative offices and the undertaker is contacted at a later time.

The remaining eight per cent of us will die elsewhere. This will include homes for the elderly, one's own home, somebody else's home, for the houseproud, that is really dying of embarrassment, accidents of various description and the unfortunate few who pass away at the hands of violence in whatever horrible form that may take.

Taking a look at the logical side of the equation, with ninety-two per cent of death occurring in hospital and a mere eight per cent collectively covering all other forms of death, a piece of advice that may now occur to the statistician is that no matter how ill you feel, the worst place to go is a hospital.

Experience shows, unfortunately, that dogged avoidance of the clinical emporium, is no escape from the 'Grim Reaper' and although you may delay the inevitable through this denial of the disinfected establishment, it merely means that many more people will pop their clogs within one, until your number is up on the outside, so please, do the decent thing when your time comes and take your place in the ward, otherwise you could be said to be responsible for the deaths of more than eleven other people in front of you.

Look at it this way, it wasn't your fault that you were born and the chances are that if you are old enough to read this, you have probably forgiven those responsible for your existence on this earth, therefore you have taken on the responsibility for your life, so accept the finishing post gracefully and you may as well do it somewhere warm and dry having been well fed and looked after, rather than cause untold aggravation, of which I am about to unfold odd truths and ditties pertaining to the eight per cent of oddballs.

"G.R. Moss, may I help you?" may sound a simple greeting to any in need of emergency service at any time.

In the middle of the night, however, when you have been making large Z's for some considerable time and had intended to have continued doing so for an indefinite period, following frivolity and bibendum on a Saturday. It can take at least three rings of the telephone to wake, remember whose house you are at and whether you should answer the phone or not, reach across whoever, carefully, so as not to disturb, remove the receiver and utter these simple lines.

As an undertaker, you are not at liberty to switch off your telephone and sleep, anytime or should you be in the middle of an argument with the missus, pick the damn thing up and say 'WADDAYOUWANT' in a heavy tone unless you can substantiate the fact that the caller has misdialled and should retry their call taking more care this time.

A memorable occasion when the 'Graham Bell Gremlin' burst into life late one evening when engaged in a preamble to a proposal of marriage and any normal person would have let it ring, I answered in my usual polite manner, only to be greeted by my brother relating tales of woe about his own marriage and the demise thereof.

Ten years later, he is divorced and remarried and I am still single. My own thoughts of nuptiality were immediately shelved and I never knew whether to hug him or hit him. I have done both since.

The first thing that the rookie remover realises about people dying in their own homes is that chances of the lift working are inversely proportional to the number of floors above ground on which the death occurred. The second thing that is very quickly learnt is that the weight of the person who has died is equal to the average weight of a person of that age multiplied by the number of floors over which the lifts are not working.

Thus, if a block has two lifts each supplying alternate floors and one is inoperative, the furthest one will have to carry the body is one floor and the deceased will remain at average weight, however, if there are two lifts not working over three floors, a frail old lady of 100 years plus can put on about six times her feeble four stone to make up to a twenty-four stone monster.

Arriving at a tower block and finding all four lifts out of order with the target residence above the tenth floor will prompt an experienced undertaker to renegotiate terms and remunerations of employment prior to starting the weary trek upward.

One of the most surprising things to most undertakers is the difference in conditions and cleanliness under which people are prepared to exist. The contrast is always most marked when having occasion to visit two different dwellings on the same estate within a short space of time. The difference between clean living and squalor seems to have very little to do with the wealth of the people involved so the removal vehicle always carried plastic over boots, shoulder length gloves, aprons as well as copious quantities of strong disinfectant.

Something that most people find most surprising is the instance of hoax removals. This is one of the most unkind things that can happen, not to mention being damned annoying for the funeral director. For the most times that the undertaker is called to a house as a hoax, it is usually a prank by children or adolescents who like to watch the undertaker turn up at some later time to frighten a friend, however sometimes, it is genuine attempt to "get even" or cause as much grief as possible.

On the initial call, the undertaker will make certain enquiries to validify the death as far as possible and small hesitations of reply and odd background noises will cause suspicion in the instances of the prankster, but the nastier variety of hoaxer is harder to fool and overconfidence of the caller may well be the reason for the undertaker's caution.

The network of camaraderie of funeral directors was such that suspicion would invoke a pattern of calls to go around the neighbourhood, warning of a possible hoax. One or two will get through every year and the poor unwitting undertakers' tale of woe will give rise to much mirth in the trade over the following few days.

One cold and windy night when I was called from a particularly pleasant evening which involved a beautiful young lady and a rather pleasant dinner and my calls were being taken by dear old Frank, we arrived at the house late at night in the rain just as a minicab drove up. I waited as the cab driver approached the house, nursing my suspicions but was taken off guard when the cab driver walked up the path of the house next door. I quickly made it to the doorway through the rain and rang the bell loudly. Over the wall, the cab driver called to me, shielding himself from the downpour.

"What number you got?"

"Thirty-six!" I replied.

"You call a cab?"

"You must be joking!" My first fears on seeing the cabby were now coming back with a vengeance, I turned round to the doorway of number thirty-six to find a very large specimen of the human race dressed in his nightclothes, an expression of fire and brimstone on his face and something resembling a baseball bat in his hands.

"FAAARRR COUGGHHH!" he said, I think, authoritatively and repeatedly, with every step advancing toward me. Not having my cap, glove or ball with me and being very unsure of the rules pertaining to nocturnal baseball, I was a mite taken aback. However, my legs, having more sense, took me smartly down the garden path as the cold rain brought a temporary halt to the night shirted bat wielder.

Meanwhile, the cabbie, having a less suspicious mind than my own, had decided that he was at the wrong doorway and had, unbeknown to me, hastened down the path of number thirty-eight and swung into the path of thirty-six at the rate of any sensible being might do in that weather. Realising the error of its own judgement, my head now decided to join in what my legs had initiated some moments before and did the normal thing of facing in the direction of movement. Wrong again!

In an instant, the cabbie's face met mine with a soggy wet 'squidge' and a 'thud'. The rain stopped, the sun came out and the church bells started to ring as the bluebirds started chirping. Momentarily, I thought, *Not a bad day*. Then reality reared its ugly head once more.

"FAAAAAAARRRRRR COUGHHHHHHHHHH!" The sun had gone, it was raining, the person who was flashing strong and multicoloured flashlights in my face had stuck a wrought-iron gate painfully under my arm whilst pushing one of my feet through one of the smaller gaps at the bottom of the gate, my other leg had been taken firmly in a half something or other and a stunned cab driver was sat on top of it.

I heard the rain scream as it was being cudgelled mercilessly by an approaching baseball bat. I was off, gate, cabbie and all. I made the van without either, jumped in and slammed the door behind me.

"Go—Go—GGooooooooooooo!" I said, in complete calmness.

"There is a car in front of us!" said Frank with an air of infuriating correctness.

"Then go the other way, damn it!" and a few choice adjectives.

"It's a one-way street," he said, with more of the same.

"Look, I'm the boss, I do the funnies and you laugh, meanwhile, get me out of here!"

Luckily, the cabbie had by now ceased his tour of the upper atmosphere, courtesy of my removing my leg from beneath him and had alighted adjacent to his vehicle and had, similar to ourselves, decided to leave without enquiring further about his fare.

"Next time you take the call, you can go to the door first, OK?"

"OK!" A new rule had been forged at our shop.

I went home, showered and slumped into bed, exhausted. That night, my slumbers were disturbed on several occasions because either the gate was jabbing my arm or the cabbie was jumping on my leg but they always disappeared before I awoke.

Apparently, during an evening when they have had calls from seventeen unsolicited cabs, four police cars, three ambulances, six insurance salesmen and an undertaker when they are trying to get some sleep before going on night shift at midnight, some people can lose their sense of humour.

After a few hoaxes at the beginning of my career when we would arrive at a house or flat, usually in the middle of the night, amidst hordes of kids riding bicycles only to find the door firmly bolted from the outside and never knowing who was responsible.

I received a call, around midnight, of course, from a young man who said that his brother had died he easily gave me his own name and telephone number and the number he was calling from. The young man who had died was the proprietor of a local sports shop who had died from leukaemia at home. He had been cared for at home by the outpatients department of the local hospice and the brother gave me all the details readily and correctly.

There was only one thing wrong. We had buried the man almost exactly two years before, hence I knew all the details to be correct. I remember that I was extremely angry and not at all polite to the caller. I have never been able to understand why anyone would want to cause someone already so tragically bereaved of a young son and husband, any more grief.

Other hoaxes are less elaborate, however, just as believable and the call may be just as plausible, explaining that the house is very run down and they live in a downstairs room, being the only inhabitable part of the house. So we happily arrive at the address, which, as warned, resembles that Addams Family residence but without the glass and hopefully without 'Spot' too. The door pushed open easily and in the gloom, the rain and gales were having a day off. I could see the flicker of a candle.

This was not usually the sort of place we would visit as a private funeral director, this was more like the job for the council contractor. A forest of dry rot turned the hallway into an eerie avenue. Carefully picking our way over rotten floorboards that were now more used as food for the flora than support to 'Hom Sap', I was very relieved to find a herd of winos huddled around the flickering light adorning the empty bottle in the middle of the floor. They were all in the best health that could be expected in view of their vocation. We left.

The only hoax when I had to genuinely laugh at having been removed from the side of my young lady and taken for a 'ride' on a very cold night and I could only think that this prank was perpetrated by some very smart students, probably medical, since they knew how to answer my "minefield" questionnaire perfectly.

I was completely taken in, we arrived at the house one Saturday night having slid in countless directions on the ice. The house was in a blaze of light, as was to be expected on such occasions when the whole family may well have gathered before my arrival. I skipped up the steps to the front door and rang the bell. It was a newly renovated house and I was expecting to be dealing with a family of above average wealth and intelligence.

The door was opened by a young man in jeans whose physique was well suited to the rugby field. He was backed up by more people of similar age and build, some holding glasses.

"Mr Lawrence?" I asked politely.

"Have you come about the body?" was the reply.

"Yes, sir!" I answered, somewhat surprised at the impersonality in his voice.

"He got better!" the door was slammed in my face amongst hoots of laughter from Mr Lawrence and his partying friends.

A little fed up, but with more than a smile on my face, we made our way home. On the way, we spotted another undertaker's van and directed him away from the party and therefore spoiled a little of their fun.

As a hoax, I found this more acceptable since it was only directed at ourselves and no malice was intended.

I arrived back at my warm bed sometime later, looking forward to a cuddle. "You're colder than death. Get away from me!" was the only response I received. I shivered to sleep, cursing the party.

A great number of people are bedridden and unable to look after themselves prior to death. What a surprise! Not many people are lucky enough to pop their clogs after a quiet pint or mowing the lawn after having sat down to a steaming cup of tea. As such, those unfortunates are unable to care for those little niceties that we all take for granted, such as cutting their toenails.

Therefore, it is often the poor luckless undertaker and his cronies that may be the first to get anywhere near the frayed ends of leg and their horny caps in many a year.

Toenails are those delicate things that parents of new-born children marvel at as having been produced so perfectly in the womb and then proceed to grow relentlessly and break annoyingly during the following years, snag tights, cut a loved one during a passionate embrace in all sorts of places and during the closing years tend to go wild and thicken, turning into grotesque miscoloured shapes defying the usual clippers and seeming as though they would be more in place on the beak of a vulture or the front of a platypus.

All this has to be removed from the bed and where do you pick up a body from, the wrists and ankles. The horny toenails will snag cuffs and plastic gloves and, as such, are fairly repulsive to the living. I have been on removals with tough men who have slopped around linoleum floor in a soup of human remains and the accompanying stench without a murmur but at the sight of the hated horny toecaps have winced, moaned and complained bitterly.

"'Ere John," everyone in East London is called John, "Can we swap ends?"

So please, if you are not feeling well, have a thought for the poor undertaker. After all, it is only a job for us. Have your toenails clipped regularly and keep your feet clean and remember, if your feet smell and your nose runs, you have been built the wrong way up.

"How are you fixed for a removal sometime today?" asked Ray, the coroner's officer.

"At your service, as usual, my old mate, who, where and when," I replied.

"Well, I'm not quite sure, but it will be today." There was a tone in his voice that betrayed a grin on his face.

"Murder?" I asked, knowing that in such cases, the forensic people take their time and then the photographer has to come and take full records before the 'Guest of Honour' is removed. It's not like Perry Mason, where the only thing to start an investigation from is a white chalk outline.

"No, well, we don't think so at present." He was being very cagey. "I thought of you immediately for this one." I could tell he was trying to conceal something from me but I didn't know what, I tried the tactful approach.

"You're hiding something Ray, it's a large one, isn't it!"

"No, not at all."

"Then it smells awful."

"No, not at all."

"Then it's floating in something nasty."

"No, not at all."

"Then it's in kit form."

"No, not at all."

"Then it's been there a very long time."

"At last," he said.

"The job will probably be later this afternoon and as far as we can tell, it's been there for about a year. What we want is someone who can move it to the mortuary without damaging it."

It may seem funny that it is possible to damage a dead body further than it has been already pursuant to passing through 'Period C' (See Chapter 1), however, after death, especially if the room is fairly clean and the person involved is underweight, the body will start to dry out. If this process continues unhindered and in dry weather conditions, the result will be a totally dehydrated corpse on which even maggots will dry out.

The downside is that some time, the body fluids will have seeped into whatever the person was lying on at the last and stick to it. Thus, any heaving about without great care will cause the body to snap into pieces. Apart from being more to pick up, it is still a particularly unpleasant thing to happen.

I gathered such information from Ray as I could, so as to be prepared. The body was very brittle but was at least on a bed, second floor in fifties built block and narrow concrete stairway. The lift was an addition, as with so many, would therefore be tiny and we would not be able to use it as standing the body upright in the shell would risk it breaking and crumpling into a little heap of rubble at the bottom of the shell. Not good.

To be prepared, I took a sheet of plywood half an inch thick and cut it to fit snugly into the bottom of the shell and drilled holes into each corner, through the two holes at each end, I threaded pieces of sash cord and knotted the underneath to provide some sort of handle so as to avoid the possibility of getting one's fingers trapped between plywood and shell and thus having to spend the afternoon as an unwilling audience to the postmortem examination.

At last, the call came through to go and collect the body. The member of staff I had with me had not been at the job for very long. We had started the job full of gusto and cocky confidence and had therefore been through all the 'puddles' that the rookie might have expected to being both physical and metaphorical.

"What's it going to be like?" he asked quizzically.

"Dead," was the only accurate reply I could give.

People new to the trade always want to know such daft things in advance and then proceed to talk incessantly about it afterwards. They proffer theories on the cause and mode of death, including how long it has been since the death occurred, usually based on some clever and memorable discovered Dick Tracey or Mike Hammer just two weeks before. The details of quantities of flies, maggots, stench and how they put their hand on something extremely unpleasant are discussed at length until someone more experienced takes the rookie firmly by the throat and quietly lets them know that it is time to cease talking on the subject.

Some years into the trade myself, I was glad that the brain cell controlling my sense of smell had provided me with a switch that would select the 'OFF' position in the proximity of death but also have the ability to detect bad beer prior to the first taste.

We arrived at the scene of the expiration and made our way between the sea of cars with blue jam jars upturned on the roof to place the vehicle as close to the entrance to the flats as possible and I made my way up the stairs to the dwelling.

I walked in to the uncarpeted two bed flat which had not seen a paintbrush for many years, old newspapers and trash was scattered all around. I found the pathologist dressed from head to toe in white plastic clothing looking more like an employee from a bacterial warfare establishment than a person someone attending the place where another had merely breathed out and forgotten what to do next.

The little old dehydrated lady was lying in the second bedroom on the bed. She must have been very slightly built during her last years but in her present state, she probably weighed about forty to fifty pounds, including the maggots.

"Nice day for it!" I said non-committally. He looked at me silently over his half glasses.

"I don't know how you are going to get this to the mortuary without breaking anything," he said after a lengthy pause.

"Nothing here worth saving," I said sarcastically and looking around.

"I'm not here to have a smashing time. But I do have a couple of ideas." My humour was greeted with contempt, a shake of the head from the pathologist.

Having weighed up the situation, I went back to the van and driver, we took the shell and 'secret' carrying board up to the flat. The stairs and front door were no problem but once inside the place, we had the problem of a tight and narrow turn before the bedroom. Leaving the shell in the hallway, we carried the board into the bedroom.

"Now I want you to be very careful," said the pathologist. "We do not have a cause of death yet."

"Well," I replied, "You can't change it now!"

I took a carpet layers knife from my pocket and noticed the enquiring looks on the faces of both pathologist and my own man. I cut the sheet and mattress cloth around the body, as I cut, the springs made 'boinging' noises as the blade passed over them, the maggots and the deceased remained silent.

"Give me a hand to break this free." I said to the driver, he was looking particularly nonplussed by the whole situation.

"Who, me?" he asked unhopefully.

"Who else?" was the obvious reply.

"That's a shame," he said, looking around.

"Well, you can always live in hope."

"What we have to do is to unstick her from the mattress." I tried to sound as nonchalant as possible, knowing that the mere thought of the reality before us was unpleasant enough and the idea of having to peel it free was worse.

"That's what I thought you were going to say," he replied resignedly.

The job was achieved without damage or chunder, so we slid the board under the body and carried it out to the shell without mishap. Once strapped inside, we started to make our way down the four half flights of stairs. In an effort to keep the shell level, the man at the foot was holding his end at shoulder height and at the head, I was bending double to maintain equilibrium. Straightening up at each landing, there was much stubbing of toes and "Steady as you go," "Easy" and "OK" before we reached the van and were off to the mortuary with our prize.

After all that and the postmortem was over, we discovered that she had died of natural causes and her brother, who was described as being "A few bricks short of a load," had been living in the same flat and had forgotten that his sister had been living with him but wondered why he had not heard from her for so long!

"She even forgot my birthday!" he was reported to have said.

The body was in a similar state at a removal handled by one of my local undertaker friends, this was also found out by the national press who had a 'Graveyard Day' with it, but they always miss something.

An elderly couple were living in a high rise estate in Hackney and the husband passed on while sitting in the chair in the living room. The old lady was either mentally unstable or was pushed to it by the death of her husband quite understandably so, however, she failed to inform anyone of the death for some months.

As with our old lady, the conditions were such that the corpse merely dehydrated where it was, in the chair.

I forget exactly how the death was discovered by the authorities but when it came to light, the old lady merely stated, "He hasn't been well, but he'll be up and about in a day or so." Totally ignoring the fact that daddy was by now completely mummified!

As usual, in these bizarre cases, the pathologist was called to the scene and made his preliminary inspection.

"I want him down at the mortuary, undamaged." This was a pretty impossible request. As the undertakers' men tried to move the old chap, the worst happened, with the result that the head fell off scattering the dried skin and bones over the floor.

The bits were carefully collected and one of the coroner's officers removed a biro from his pocket and collected the vertebrae of the neck on this convenient stick.

On arrival at the mortuary, the body was placed on the table for the pathologist's inspection.

"We did the best we could but he broke at the neck," the officer told the pathologist convincingly.

The pathologist took one look at the damaged area. "Funny, isn't it that this man has gone through his entire life with his vertebrae in the wrong order!"

"Can you do a removal from the hospital first thing on Monday morning?" asked Ray one Saturday.

"Yes, no problem," I replied, taking the details.

"The wife is on her way up to you to make arrangements. Get TWO chairs ready!" he said.

"You're trying to tell me something, Ray, aren't you?"

"What I'm telling you is to get TWO chairs ready."

"Strong ones?"

"STRONG ones."

"And she hasn't got a friend with her, has she?"

"No."

"I get the drift," I said, wondering what to expect.

Some moments later, the woman, Mrs Pettit, arrived. No more than five feet two inches across the hips and a little shorter. I listened carefully as our chairs groaned while we discussed the arrangements for her late husband, thankfully a much less voluminous person and the funeral was carried out with Mrs Pettit taking more than her fair share of seats in both car and church, otherwise without ado.

A year or so later, Frank was telephone sitting for an evening and my pager bleeped accursedly from my pocket. I called back.

"We've got a removal and I can't raise anyone but you," he said apologetically.

"Sorry to disturb your dinner," he added.

"OK, Frank, where is it and I'll meet you there in about an hour?"

This would give me time to finish my dinner and get back to Hackney. As he gave me the address, I began to cast my mind back and both number and street name seemed familiar.

"I think we've done for the family before," concluded Frank.

"Pettit," I said.

"Yes, that's right," he said.

"How did you know?"

"Mrs Daphne Pettit."

"Yes, but how did you know and what's that got to do with?"

"Well, I'll tell you. If we are going to move Mrs Daphne Pettit from her bedroom in that house, two of us ain't goin to be enough!"

Luckily, my memory for people, places and names is excellent and saved us more than a little embarrassment on this occasion.

Another place popular for death is the "Home for the Unhinged," the place where people who think differently to most of us or those who don't quite fit into society are placed under various degrees of confinement. Since these places are often termed "hospitals" and have a number of inmates will remain within the walls until they are called to the great marble store in the sky. Therefore, the collection of the body is made from this establishment.

On arrival at the gate, we were met by the security guard.

"Drive up to the main entrance, 'admin' is at the end of the corridor, last door on the left, mate," directed by the guard. "Don't talk to anyone but the staff," he said.

We drove up to the main entrance of this imposing Victorian building through the beautifully kept gardens and lawns. Various people were doing gardening and walking about things in the vast acreage of the estate which was once surrounded by woodland but now ringed by housing estates forming London's sprawling suburbs.

"Is there anyone here to tell us who are the staff and who are the inmates," asked Porky pensively.

"Furthermore," he enquired with an openhanded gesture, "Should we ask one of the inmates whether he was staff or not, would he tell us the truth and would we know if that were the truth or not. Do we have a lie detector on board?"

"'Fraid not," was the only reply I could think of in view of his unarguable logic.

"If we're going to be doing much more work out of here, it might be a worthwhile investment. They all look the same to me."

We discussed that silly story about the two guards in front of the two doors, one of which led to hell and one to heaven, when one of the guards spoke the truth and the other lied and only having one question to ask. Neither of us could remember the question to ask or what it would inform us anyway. Also, there was always the chance that the person who was supposed to lie would tell the truth in real life.

"Well, that got us nowhere," said Porky. We arrived at the imposing front door.

"It passed the time between that front gate and front door," I pointed out. "You wait here and I'll go and get the paperwork."

"What, on my own?"

"Yes, you're a big boy now."

"Can I lock the doors?"

"Yes, if you must." I had reached the top of the steps and opened the door.

"Mr Watson?" said Porky pathetically.

"What is it now?"

"Don't be long," he asked. Porky was always overdramatizing but this time he made me shudder. Well, you never do know about these places.

I found the office and the assistant called the mortuary keeper and stamped my removal order. I signed the register. "We keep the register in here so there will be nothing to sign at the mortuary, the removal order will suffice. The mortuary keeper will meet you outside," all said with a cheery smile.

I bade her thanks and made my way back down the long, high and uncarpeted corridor, my footsteps echoing all around. I reached the front door again and my footsteps caught up with me.

Porky's little smiling face was beaming at me through the driver's window and there was a white-coated person sitting next to him. I walked round to the passenger side and opened the door.

"That was quick," I said. "You will have to direct us to the mortuary, we've never been here before."

"I know," said the white-coated man. "I was just talking to your mate here!" he waved a hand in a general direction and Porky started off.

The waves occurred at various intersections in the driveways and through the gardens with dear Porky trying his best to interpret them. The monotone of moaning from this man was more than one might expect from the average mortuary keeper, however, this was no ordinary hospital. We then arrived at the small brick built building well away from the main building with the telltale double doors and 'wheelchair' ramp. I gave the removal order to the white-coated man.

"George Henry Walker," said the man, "Oh, that was a nutter if ever I saw one."

We all got out and the man reached up under a concealed eave of the low building and produced a very large and very old key that looked as if it should have been dangling from the belt of a gaoler in the Bastille. The key was fed into the lock and turned with a satisfying 'clonk'. Porky had opened the back doors of the van and removed shell and trolley whilst the man and I had entered the mortuary. Small clean, with only three trays in one refrigerator unit.

As he opened the door of the fridge, the cooling fan came to a stop with a "tink, tink, tink," as the blades touched the dusty wire mesh guard protecting it from I know not what.

"Bloody nutter!" muttered the man. Porky and I said nothing but we caught each other's eye with an enquiring frown.

"Bloody nutter!" he said loudly as he slid the tray onto the trolley with a crash.

We unwrapped the body and checked the name on the ankle and lifted him into the shell without a word. The white-coated man slammed the tray back into the refrigerator unceremoniously and kicked the door closed with a large, grubby boot. He held his hand out for the customary tip, eyes cast down. Porky was pushing the shell into the back of the van as the man looked up straight into my eyes.

"Is it a burial or cremation?" he enquired in a gravelly voice.

"Burial," I replied.

"Pity, I like it when they burn 'em," he said despondently.

Porks and I looked at each other, wondering about the two guards and whether it was worth trying to ask any questions at all. In a flash, we had the back doors of the van closed and ourselves in the front. With the slam of the two doors and a spin of the starter, we were off toward the main gate.

"Are you thinking what I'm thinking?" asked Porky.

"Well, I'm thinking, 'Do you know your way back to the main gate'," as we sped through the grounds.

"Hopefully," was the best reply I could get.

"Where did you find him?" I asked.

"He just walked up and asked if I was the undertaker."

"So there you were in this van in a hospital grounds, wearing a black suit, white shirt and black tie. You're not a greengrocer, are you?"

"Well, I assumed that he was the mortuary keeper as he just got in the van and started asking if I had been there before and whether I knew where the mortuary was."

We arrived safely at the gate and passed through only after the security guard had had a good look in the back.

"Alright, lads?"

"Yup!" we said, neither of us even wanting to know whether the white-coated man was staff or inmate.

"We will never know if we've got to be thankful or not," said Porky reflectively.

"That's just fine by me!" I retorted.

"That's just fine by me!"

It was a bright, sunny Sunday morning in late September and London was still reeling under the shock of a good summer, late though it had been in starting but it had turned out to be very hot.

People had been lazing around in the parks and commons, eating, drinking and getting on with all those other things that people generally do in life, like dying.

I was still in my robe but catching up on some well overdue paperwork in the office, it was sometimes handy, living on the premises and journey time to and from work was therefore kept to a minimum. At about twenty past eleven when the telephone rang.

"G.R. Moss, may I help you?" I enquired politely, just longing to say something like, what the hell do you want?

"What are you doing?" came a voice through the instrument.

"Well, I'm sitting here in my bathrobe being interrupted by some nut who has nothing to do but ask daft questions of people trying to catch up on some work with one eye on the clock and looking forward to the bewitching midday hour when wonderland reopens its doors. Good Morning Ray and I hope it's what I can do for you that is on your mind at the moment." Well, at least there could be some work in the offing.

"How are you fixed for a quick one?"

"Another daft question, you always know that I'm ready for anyone to buy me a pint. I think that a great number of people in this country fail to understand the love, care and sheer hard work that goes into the creation of good English beer."

"A nice idea, but I actually meant a removal!"

"No problem. Where and who?" I wrote down the details, bade Ray a goodbye and kind regards to his wife, who was still a great cook and said that we should get together again soon.

I rang round and found Ed. It was a good thing that it was before twelve because it would have been much more difficult to find him after that time.

"We've got one, fancy doing it and I will buy you a pint afterwards, in the pub by twelve if we're lucky."

"See you in five."

"Fine."

Ed arrived and changed into his suit and we were off in a few minutes more. We did not have far to go, the estate was visible from the back gate of the garage, so we arrived in mere minutes.

"This is handy," said Ed. "I hope the lift works." It was, so we naturally assumed that all was well upstairs. The lift door made the usual grinding noise as they closed. Ed and I stood in the gloom as the lift clanked its way uncertainly upward until it arrived at the desired floor with a bump, the door ground its way open.

A policeman stood protectively in front of one of the four doors that led from the central shaft of the twenty-two floor tower block.

"Uh, oh!" said Ed with a look of foreboding on his face. "I see a bad omen before me. Is there something that you have not informed me of?" he was looking at me, his face set in a frown.

The reason for this frown was quite valid since the average policeman will be far happier sat comfortably in a flat or house waiting for the undertakers arrival and thus avoiding all enquiries from nosey neighbours, unless, the interior of the flat is an unpleasant, dirty or otherwise smelly place to be.

The policeman had a glum look on his face and our suspicions rose further.

"You've got a surprise coming," said the policeman, tossing his head back in the direction of the door behind him.

"Give us a clue," said Ed. "Is it a nice or a nasty one."

A wicked grin on his face. We had seen and dealt with easy and difficult jobs in our time and we're both prepared to take the rough with the smooth and there was no point in being anything but cheerful about the job. The policeman pushed the door open to let us in, I noticed that there was an immediate left turn inside the door as the bobby confirmed.

"It's a bit of a tight turn and I don't know whether you will get that through," he said nodding at the shell and added, "I should leave that out here."

I decided against telling him that we knew what we were doing, as a little voice inside me was telling tales of warning. Against my better instincts, I left the shell out in the lobby. I was always aware of the habit of coincidences and feared some poor old person having just lost their loved one would be living on the same level and choose that precise moment to open their front door or arrive by lift. I left Ed on the landing with the shell and went in with the policeman.

The walls were painted with a blue grey emulsion, the floor was uncarpeted, the kitchen and bathroom were not exactly clean but I had seen worse, I walked into the living room. The blue grey theme ran through this room too with dingy curtains hanging over the blue grey dust covered glass, the furniture was well-worn, unmatching but could have seen a few more days, though now, probably wouldn't.

In front of one of the armchairs was a large whale like creature that had once been a human being dressed in what could only be described by anyone of less a stature than Schwarzenegger, as a tent.

I looked at the policeman and back at the whale and back, again, at the policeman.

"That," I remarked, "Must have been a very high tide!"

He laughed.

"I don't know what you fellahs are going to do but it seems to me as though you have got one hell of a job on your hands."

"We!" I corrected.

"Not me mate, I'm getting no nearer that than I am now!" Standing firmly in the doorway.

"You may change your mind if I were to point out that you can leave the place once she has," I said, pointing whalewards. "However, not before. It could take me quite some time before I find another member of my staff to assist. There again, one quick heave and you get a lift back to the nick, all done and back for lunch."

This was said with as much conviction as possible. Although all police officers are taught to handle a dead body and they sometimes encounter particularly grizzly examples, there are some who positively dislike the fact of having to do so, this I respected and seldom asked for help. This occasion, I needed help and knew it but only in the initial stages. Once loaded on the trolley, Ed and I would be able to handle it the rest of the way.

"I hope you've got some gloves for me," he replied with a glum resignation in his voice.

"We can do better than that," I said cheerfully, "gloves, bib, overboots and—and a peg, if you want."

I sent Ed down for an additional pair of disposable gloves, for ourselves we usually carried such things in our pockets from the van to the scene, from where, they usually travelled with the body until disposed of. I prepared the stretcher and when Ed returned, we rolled the whale about, slid the stretcher in underneath and rolled her back on to it.

Strapped in and covered as much as possible, we lifted, in an effort to lift the body high enough to put it on the trolley and then to wheel it out to the shell outside.

"Someone has nailed this to the floor!" I said as the stretcher merely bent and, although we were standing upright with handles at hip level, the centre of the stretcher remained firmly on the floor. The officer had, meanwhile, been hiding conveniently in the lavatory.

"We are going to need your help here," I shouted as the flush quietened.

"On my way," came the gracious, though reluctant, reply.

"OK mate, what we have here is a problem and it's going to take all three of us to solve it. Move the armchair out, put the trolley against the wall and then we can slide the whale over to the trolley, then the wall will stop it running away."

With this accomplished, we began to lift, the policeman at one end, Ed at the other and me at the handles in the middle. We heaved and strained until about three quarters of the assembled crowd were huffing and puffing and the whole lot red faced. It is noteworthy that only one present who had not taken a single breath during the entire proceedings had the reddest face of all and would continue to do so for some time. At last, we managed to slide the stretcher onto the trolley.

"Well done," I panted at the others. "Well done. It's all more of the same from here," I added, to boost morale.

We checked the lobby for neighbours and any other nosey sort that might be passing then pushed the wheeled whale out through the front door.

"Do you think that we could be lucky enough to not be interrupted if we were to try and take her off the stretcher and into the shell, otherwise she might get stuck and trap our stretcher."

"A good thought Ed," said I. "Officer, would you kindly do police-like duties and stop anyone from coming out of any of those three front doors or either of the two lifts whilst we, er, do what he said," pointing at Ed.

The officer, suitably impressed at the impossibility of the task, smiled and said, "No problem," with more than the slightest tone of sarcasm.

"He's getting good enough to work for us," Ed said dryly.

Our guard guarded whilst we unwrapped, heaved and hoped for solitude. The whale wobbled and, with a final heave from us both, flopped unceremoniously into the groaning shell and quivered like some grotesque, gigantic jelly.

"I hope the shell stands up to it, that sounded like a nasty crack as she went in there," offered Ed.

"Shut up, hope for the best and I hope you remembered your prayers last night."

"Oh, I prayed all evening, guvnor, but she still said no! Strange creatures, women," said Ed reflectively.

The whale lay in the shell, its huge belly, covered in tent, upward and protruding above the top of the shell like dough of a well-risen loaf in a bread tin. There was no way in which we were going to be able to get the lid on.

"Only one thing to do," I said, "grab a cover or blanket from the old dear's flat and cover her up with it, when we get to the mortuary, we can back right in but we will have to risk it here," referring to the trip from the lift to the van.

The whale was now, again, off the trolley and the heaving, huffing and puffing resumed until the whale, this time in the shell and much more manageable, was back on wheels.

The lift passed by our floor on several occasions and we had held our breath, wondering what the policeman would do if the door had opened at our level. The policeman locked the door of the flat as we tidied up the stretcher and with the temporarily redundant lid clutched against the side of the shell, we rolled our charge into the lift with its covered mountain of flesh wobbling like a water bed on wheels, we both tried not to look at it or each other.

"Nice day for it," said Ed as the door ground to a close and we were left in the gloom.

"Yes," I replied, leaving the situation completely open.

"What?" the officer bit the bait with the naïve look on his face.

"Wine, women and song." chirps Ed.

"If I'm buying you a pint after this, you are not going to sing and you can find your own woman." I shuddered as Ed was now in the mood to make fun of the officer so I butted in quickly.

"Need a lift back to the nick," I asked.

"Very nice of you," he replied.

The lift arrived at the ground floor and the door made their usual complaint about moving and we pushed our prize along the paved path as ripples ran rhythmically over the quivering mass in time to the bump of the wheel between the slabs. We felt lucky that we had not passed anyone with our macabre mobile mountain of matter, we soon had the whole thing locked in the back of the van and were on our way to the police station to drop the bobby and collect the mortuary keys.

We stopped outside; I jumped out and held the door for our helpful officer, who looked at me enquiringly.

"I'm not from here, I'm from Stoke Newington. I wondered why you were coming this way. Now I'm further away than when we started."

"Oh, is that so? I'm sorry. Well, we'll give you a run over there after we have dropped the body off at the mortuary," I said with as much surprise in my voice as I could muster.

The borders between territories of police stations are as odd and confusing as any English parish or county boundary. I looked over at Ed, who was obviously staring in the other direction, trying to avoid my eye and went into the station for the keys.

"That was quick," said Ed as I returned.

"Boring day apparently, no murders, muggings, fires or car smashes." I closed the door of the van and we were off round the corner to the mortuary.

"This officer says that the Nightingale Estate is on Stoke Newington's patch and so is our shop," Ed sparked up.

"Is that so?" I replied, looking out of the side window, hiding a smile. "How long has that been, mate?" I asked.

"As long as I've been here," he replied.

"Well, now, you're here, you may as well give us a hand and we'll all be out of here quicker," I said cheerfully.

Hesitantly, the officer followed us into the mortuary and helped us with the whale wobbling. We had to leave the bale of blubber on the mortuary table as it would not fit onto the fridge and I called Ray.

"You should see the size of it, we've had to leave it on the table. Was there something that you should have told me?" I asked suspiciously.

"No, I don't think so," came the reply quite convincingly, though I was never sure with Ray.

Meanwhile, Ed had reloaded the van and managed to 'steal' a body on the way.

"Picked up Parsons while we were there. That will save us a trip tomorrow morning," he said happily as we drove off to drop off to the next nick to drop our little helper.

"One of these days they're going to rumble you on that one," said Ed after the officer was safely out of earshot.

"They haven't yet, Cor, have you seen the time, we had better get straight to the boozer after we have parked up it's nearly one thirty." This being the bad old days when pubs shut at two in the afternoon on Sundays. "That took us nearly two hours."

"Here's to removals being paid by the pound and coppers remaining as gullible as they are. Cheers!" said Ed as the well-earned amber ale slipped away.

During my early days in the trade when my mother's, father's, brother's, son's, wife's, sister's husband was still manager, I arrived at the shop early one morning to be told that we had to go out straight away to do a removal, collect the keys to the house from the police station and take an old tramp into our chapel, he, unusually had seen a doctor within the required length of time.

We quickly made ready, collected the keys and arrived at the house in a short time. We had been told that the body was in the downstairs bathroom of the living (strange name for this one now) room. I am still unsure how the doctor and police managed to get into the room, as we had to push the body back with the door before we could get into the room.

It would have been natural to assume that the body had just slumped back against the door and pushed it closed again. If this had been the case, why didn't they move the body away from the door? When we pushed the door, however, it still left only just enough room for me to get in and I was not exactly overweight.

After some amount of heaving and grunting, I managed to pull the old fellah up enough so that Bob could open the door fully and then we took the body out easily past the roomful of decaying food in its various states of decomposition and back to our chapel.

The tramp was dressed in scruffy old clothes and we left him, head propped up, in the shell in our chapel until his daughter arrived to make the arrangements for the funeral. It was to be a simple burial where only two or three mourners were expected to attend. After finalising details, the daughter asked if we had found any money with her father as she said that he had always carried his cash. The police had not mentioned any and so we went to the chapel to search.

In his pockets we found over four hundred pounds in cash, all in neatly folded clean notes. Quite a surprise. The cost of a funeral at that time was less than three hundred pounds so the daughter paid the account in advance and took the balance with her.

It is very often very surprising how much cash some people carry, especially those one would least expect to have it.

Then there was Carol. We met whilst she was making the arrangements for the funeral of one of her residents. Carol ran a sheltered accommodation block for the local borough. We had met some years before; however, she called me on behalf of one of her elderly residents. Ellen Brown, who wanted to make arrangements for her funeral before her death. This is not a common practice but it does happen.

Ellen was fairly elderly and had a speech impediment that made our meeting somewhat difficult. She had been a funeral director's receptionist when she had worked and had thoroughly enjoyed the job, meeting people and doing something unique to them. Her quiet calm and assurance would have made her excellent for the job, together with just the right amount of humour.

A few months later, when I met Carol again, we decided that it was a little unfair to her residents to have to wait for one of them to die before we could meet again so we arranged to meet for a drink, dinner and things went from there.

Local undertakers' noses were suitably put out of joint by this state of affairs but we took the view that this was their problem, not ours.

Carol, being in the trade, was not put off by the idea of death or the sight of a dead body, also for a slightly built five foot nothing, she was very strong. One evening, when the phone rang whilst we were together and it was work. I was one member of staff short anyway and unable to find the another it was too late to call out Bob, the old manager.

"I'll come," said Carol.

I didn't dare say that she would not be strong enough or refuse her offer in such a liberated world. However, I did wonder what the relatives would think when we arrived.

"There's nothing that would worry me," she added cheerfully. However, I think I would have still fought shy of taking her on one of the more grizzly jobs.

We made the van ready and just as we were about to leave, the telephone rang again, yet another removal.

"One more for the Hat Trick!" I said as we left.

The first job was upstairs in a house with a winding staircase and a fairly large man, much bigger than the average. I went back to the van and Carol. "Bit of a nuisance, but we'll have to use the stretcher on this one and hope for the best with the next."

We carried two shells in the van but only one stretcher and once used it would usually be placed inside a shell, making it rather difficult, should we need it on a second job. Taking the trolley to the front door and leaving it outside, I explained.

"When we come out, you will be at the foot, so if you just walk down the path a little, I will slide the trolley underneath and then we are all set. He's quite a lump so say if you don't think you will be able to manage it."

Then I realised she was wearing high heels and though not exactly tight, a contour following skirt. "Are you going to be alright wearing those?" I added in disbelief.

"Yes, I think so," she replied confidently.

We made our way upstairs to the bedroom and I saw Carol's face as she spotted the monster.

"Are you sure?" I whispered.

"Oh, yes," she said calmly, "He looks just as if he's sleeping."

"He must be twice your weight," I pointed out.

"Well, I hope you're going to carry at least half of him and I can carry my half!" We were both whispering since the relatives were in the room next door and I was still unsure how they would react to a woman on the removal and as yet, they had not seen her.

Getting the body off the bed and onto the stretcher was the first job. Since legs are easier to handle than arms, I put Carol, all seven stone something of her, at the foot and grabbing the body firmly under the arms, I nodded to her indicating that I was ready when she was.

"Ready?" I asked. She nodded.

"OK, now!" I said quietly. It was fairly obvious to me that I was in fact doing most of the moving, however, I realised that if I kept lifting and pulling, the large man's posterior would arrive at the edge of the bed and we would be able to lower him to the floor, then in the stretcher, he would be more manageable, having handles in more useful places.

The posterior was on the very edge of the bed and we would soon be lowering the body to the floor, albeit maybe with a little bump. Just an instant before we took the weight, I realised what might happen and it did.

Although I had a firm grip of the body from under the armpits and was standing virtually over the body, Carol had a grip of the feet and with her arms at full stretch, was pulling as hard as she could. As the bottom fell off the bed, the corpse naturally bent in the middle, as it did so, it swung toward me, bringing the legs and Carol closer. The posterior hit the floor with a loud bump and the legs stopped moving. Carol, however, did not. With a rush, she cannoned into me and my end of the body, to which I was still clinging.

Somehow, we managed to avoid bursting into laughter and injury. After strapping the gent in, we now had the voyage to the van to contend with. Carol again at the foot, taking tiny steps, part of the front of her skirt hitched up by the end of the stretcher, a look of grim determination on her face as we approached the stair. We stopped briefly for a rest.

"Are you sure about this?" I asked. "Because we can go back now but not once we start down the stairs."

She nodded an OK to me and we started off again. We now slid the stretcher down the stairs with Carol making sure that the foot didn't catch anywhere and me acting as anchorman, one hand holding the two handles of the stretcher, the other taking a firm grasp of the banister rail behind me and generally stopping this great weight from chasing Carol down the stair and impaling her on the table in the hall which was to be our next problem.

The table, quite ancient, large but flimsy looking, only left a square about the width of the staircase for us to turn the body a sharp left and immediate right to reach the front door. I was about to remind dear Carol of the presence of the table when her bottom came into contact with it causing the bulging letter rack, presumably full of bills, to fall on the floor and the various knickknacks given by distant relatives on their holidays to Bognor or Bangor to shoot about the surface, the more fragile ones doing their shooting closest to the edge of the table.

During this moment of time, Carol let go of the stretcher and instinctively swung around to save the scurrying 'valuables' and in doing so, let the full weight of the body and stretcher fall onto my one hand with a jolt, my ankle turned sideways under this unexpected shock and slid noisily down a few steps, my other leg was in no place to do any supporting of such weight at the time and merely collapsed.

Somehow I managed, more by luck than judgment, to maintain my grip on both handles and rail and the result was the straightest possible line between these two points, my torso facing the banisters with my one leg underneath, the other, under the stretcher.

The body had only slipped about a foot during this endless, noisy eternity but before coming to rest, had given Carol a hefty push. This had caused her to fall gracefully sideways over the foot of the stretcher and end up on her bottom on the hall floor, legs akimbo, knickknacks rattled precariously again.

There were now three things that we could do. One, to laugh at the situation, two, scream in accordance to the pain that we had just received and three, keep absolutely silent. Luckily, there were three of us. Carol and I took our lead from the one who had just said 'BUMP' and would have appeared to be not amused, had we uncovered his face.

"You OK?" I asked in a controlled whisper, bubbles of laughter bouncing around my belly.

"Yes." She was getting to her feet.

"Have a quick look and see if we woke him up." I said, nodding to the stretcher, smiling.

There was a pregnant pause before she looked at me and said, "You have a rotten sense of humour!"

Slowly, we extracted ourselves from our immediate predicament and took stock of what we had left. Another predicament! I noticed that Carol's face had changed to a look of open-mouthed amazement, her eyes fixed at the top of the stairway behind me. I looked round, the son was standing there. The look of worry on his face soon turned to a smile and then a giggle. I wondered how long he had been there as he politely asked, "Are you OK?"

"Yes, I'm sorry, I slipped," I replied apologetically.

"Dad's a big man, isn't he and these stairs are a bit cramped. Anything I can do?"

"I don't think so, sir. It's easier from here, I hope," I replied.

We were then spurred to get on with it and after making the necessary heaves and hauling to manoeuvre the tight turns, we picked up our ends and made for the front door. Once outside, the son kindly pushed the trolley underneath the stretcher and helped us the remainder of the way.

After a few words of information and many more of apology to the son, we were on our way to what lay ahead.

At Wayman Court, a tower block, I left Carol in the van whilst I discovered that the lift we wanted was out of order, the alternative served the floors above and below, I went up to meet the relatives and sort out what we needed for this one. Thankfully, another clean and tidy flat and a poor little emaciated creature beautifully laid out on crisp clean sheets.

"Were you a nurse?" I asked the woman as we stood at the bedside whilst I removed a single gold signet ring and placed it on the table.

"During the war," she replied. "He was my lodger for fifteen years, a lovely man. He moved in to keep me company after my husband died. He helped me look after Jim before he went. He was a lovely man."

I spent a few more minutes with her as I quietly ushered her to the next room and explained what I would be doing and what she would have to do the following day.

I made my way down the one flight of stairs, the remainder of the way by lift and out to the car park to Carol. As I approached the van, I dropped my head slightly and shook it.

"What's the matter?" she said as she got out to meet me.

"You thought the last one was big," I said, straight faced.

"WHAT?" with a look of horror.

"And the lift doesn't go all the way, we'll have to use the shell." I was trying to avoid direct eye contact and thought I would soon be rumbled. But not so.

We took the trolley and shell to the serviceable lift and went up to the floor above where the body was and man—person handled our equipment down a floor. Finally, we entered the room.

"But you said he was bigger than the last one," she blurted out in a shrill voice, without thinking where she was.

"Hush up, remember where you are." Slightly embarrassed, we carried out the job and left. Another day over.

Chapter Thirteen
D.I.Y. in Death?

The whole United Kingdom has been suffering under the 'Do-It-Yourself' craze for many years and there are now a great number of specialist stores catering for the needs of DIY decorators, carpenters, plumbers, kitchen fitters and a whole host more these, as such pose no advantage, disadvantage or threat to the funeral director, however, some advantage has been gained from some DIY fields especially from electrical, roofing and car mechanics, when we have had to make arrangements for the accidental deaths resulting from those activities.

It is usually a shock to most to find out that some people actually arrange and carry out the funeral for their nearest and dearest. I do not think that this practice will have a great effect on the funeral trade as a whole or give rise to large stores opening at strategic points throughout the country supplying flat pack coffins, disposable removal stretchers and renting suitably modified Volvo estate cars in a range of suitably sombre colours.

Should this ever happen, and you find yourself in the market for a second-hand, low-mileage Volvo estate car, it might be an idea to check three things before buying if you are at all superstitious.

1. That the back seats do actually fold up.
2. Look for an abundance of dead petals under those seats.
3. The presence of rear passenger doors. It should have them.

Two other points that might arouse some suspicion are the presence of decorated glass in the rear windows or a small badge somewhere on the car stating 'Onest 'Arry's 'Earst 'Ire, 'Ackney or similar, and sold to you by someone called Fred.

The following is an edited account of an article published in the London Evening Standard on 30 November 1987 that I found most worrying. The account of the death and disposal of the late Mr Nigel Spottiswoode. It was entitled 'A Matter of Love and Death'. My reply was self-explanatory but not published to my knowledge.

During the December 1986, it was discovered that Jane's husband Nigel was suffering from cancer of the lungs and would die within a fairly short space of time; they had, between themselves, decided that they did not wish to spend money on a lavish funeral but to have a good party for the surviving spouse and friends.

With the reality of death coming closer, they managed to find someone to supply them with a coffin for the dearly, although not quite departed and, in good time, arranged the journey from North Wales to Stoke on Trent to collect the coffin. The carriage of the coffin was courtesy of the 'friend with the Volvo'. It was delivered after dark and stored in the attic until needed. This ended up as being sometime in the following May.

Nigel passed away peacefully in a nursing home with all his friends around him, and this is where the fun started. They realised that they had neither the equipment nor the experience to move Nigel from the room since it was not possible to manoeuvre the coffin out of the room in the horizontal position so they strapped him to a commode and bumped him down the fire escape.

Nigel then spent the next day in the spare room at their home before Jane realised that it would not be possible to arrange the cremation until the following Wednesday. A problem arose, presumably a matter of decomposition, something that had not been too well planned for in the previous five months and Nigel was whisked off to a local public mortuary via the window and rosebed and the timely arrival of the Volvo. This all achieved at 3 o'clock in the afternoon without a thought of what the neighbours might have in the way of feelings.

The day of the funeral arrived and again the Volvo ventured valiantly forth for the final fling. This time, with a piece of board thrown in the back for ease of loading and unloading, they were learning fast but not thinking.

On the trip to the crematorium, they discovered that the ease of 'Woode sliding on wood not only applied to the fore-and-aft movement but also side to side, what a surprise, and Nigel spent the first part of the journey slapping around merrily in the back of the estate car until another member of the 'Carry on Cortege' came up with a couple of handy briefcases to wedge 'Woode. They then arrived at the crematorium and carried out the funeral service in accordance with their own wishes, as could have been arranged, anyway.

Jane then boasts that the funeral "out of pocket" expenses were under £150.00 as compared with £500.00 to £1,000 if it had been conducted through a funeral director.

The article then continues in the vein that Jane would now wish to see DIY centres stocking flatpack coffins with A to Z instructions for assembly at home.

The article also contained various references to the fact that undertakers are now referred to as funeral directors, giving the impression that this is some sort of trend toward elitism and the wide-eyed attitude of undertakers at the crematorium when the 'Carry on Cortege' arrived.

My reply to the editor was as follows:

Dear sir,

With reference to your centre page article on Monday, 30 November, which could easily have been retitled *A Matter of Chaos after Death* or have we merely experienced a preview of Eric Sykes' much awaited sequel to *The Plank*.

As a fifth-generation funeral director, I am becoming more and more tired of this DIY and "that sounds a lot of money" attitude to our profession by people who still seem to believe in the 'Bogeyman'. I would like to dispel some myths about ourselves and our staff. We are not as crusty and dusty as you may think, we are normal human beings who happen to earn a living by disposing of the mortal remains of their fellow human beings when they have no further use for them. Indeed, you may well sit next to one at the cinema.

Tragically, Mrs Spottiswoode lost her nearest and dearest at an unusual age. This, however, gives her no right to abuse her privileged position to have a tilt at funeral directors in general. Has she no compassion for her fellow bereaved, this woman has not only her health and strength but also her friends and time, not, of course, forgetting the Volvo.

Whilst waving her banner of victory, she forgets the lone pensioner without the abilities to carry out the necessary. Can you imagine the supermarkets with little old ladies pushing trolleys around the aisles with their husband's coffin and clutching the latest edition of 'Disposing of Dorian' and the queues at the bus stops would be even more macabre.

I have no objection to people making their own arrangements for their relatives' funerals, but will they ever stop shouting about the fact that it only cost them £150.00, without including their own time at equity rates, excluding the repeat fees, the time spent by their friends assisting and the cost of the inevitable Volvo.

As I see it, the funeral, as described, has all the dignity of the first rehearsal of a Brian Rix farce.

The removal from the nursing home could have easily been executed by two trained men with a little equipment, quickly, quietly and with dignity, instead of the strapped-in, sitting on and shinning down the fire escape with little or no regard to the other residents of the home.

As I read on, it was obvious that no one had been seriously "Making Plans for Nigel," as one might have expected in view of their previously arranged pact.

Had the funeral been arranged with the services of a sympathetic funeral director, the paperwork would have been completed without the trauma as experienced and with the services of a competent embalmer, Nigel could have easily remained at home for the intervening six days before the funeral, rather than being locked away in the public mortuary for the week.

The funeral itself was obviously no better planned with Nigel careering around in the back of the Volvo until halted by two very dignified briefcases. Can you actually wonder at the undertakers' attitude at the crematorium on seeing this 'Cortege' approach? It can sometimes take a great deal of concentration to keep a straight face.

Funeral Directors, Undertakers, Human Disposal Consultants, Turf Accountants, Bookmakers, Driver, Pilot, Double Glazing Salesman, Draught Excluder, Hearse, Volvo? What's in a name? Does it matter as long as people do not end up in a chemist asking for a copy of the Evening Standard?

As most funeral directors, I am proud, very proud of the service I provide. I am part of the local community, as are the butcher, the baker and the person who runs the lighting emporium. We pay a doctor when we are ill, a plumber when we have a leak, so why is it so difficult to accept the services of the funeral director after a bereavement? Nobody wants to be ill or have a leaky pipe, few, also want to die, the choice is not ours.

Our profession is not only a service industry but also a High Street business, we have our rates and staff to pay on a full-time basis. Unfortunately, people do not always die at convenient times and places so there is also a 24 hour service to be maintained. There is much more to the job than most people realise.

I think it is about time that we cast aside the childish ideas of the nasty man in a black hat who took Granny away. We provide the community with an important service at a reasonable price and protect them from contagious diseases and unpleasantness that could easily offend.

We do not ask for applause, just the common respect that you would normally afford to your newsagent or grocer.

Yours faithfully.

Taking the cost factor and adding the time spent by friends at a reasonable hourly rate and adding the hire of the Volvo on three separate days, even forgetting the trip to Stoke-on-Trent to collect the coffin, the actual cost of carrying out this funeral would have far exceeded the £500.00 mentioned at the lower end of the scale. Our company records show the costs of funerals going back for many years and the relative cost of the service has, in fact, reduced in recent years, as have a number of services we take for granted.

It would be a shame to see an abundance of Do-it-yourself funeral facilities opening around the country and allowing people to conduct the 'easier' end of the market funerals and drive up the prices to those who do not possess the abilities, whether physical or emotional, to carry out their own service.

In general, funeral directors are a happy bunch of people who provide an exceptional service within the community with grace and style and have been described as being the last great showmen on earth.

Maybe the next thing I should write should be entitled "Disposing of Dorian," "Have Fun Frying Father!" or even "Burials without Bother."

OH WELL, SEE YOU AT THE CREMATORIUM FOR A LAST SMOKE!

_____

The Po'face
(or Postface)

American television programs have been infiltrating the British screens for many years now with a variety of soaps including those concerned with hospital and medical teams and their heroic adventures. I have noticed that they, over there, have some different terminologies and abbreviations as well as driving on the wrong (right) side of the road.

One important difference in hospitals concern the abbreviations 'B.I.D.' and 'D.O.A.' In Britain, they are short for 'Brought in Dead' and 'Date of Admission'; both terms are synonymous if you are; however, if you aren't, then only the latter applies. In America, things are slightly different where 'D.O.A.' is the abbreviation for 'Dead on Arrival'.

If, therefore, you wake up unexpectedly in a strange place and find a tag on your wrist giving various details including an entry next to the legend D.O.A., there may not be cause for alarm, provided that you can remember what country you are in, be sure about it and also remember all the above details.

If you cannot,

<u>PANIC!</u>